Henry Adolphus Miles

The Birth of Jesus

Henry Adolphus Miles

The Birth of Jesus

ISBN/EAN: 9783337771065

Printed in Europe, USA, Canada, Australia, Japan

Cover: Foto ©Lupo / pixelio.de

More available books at **www.hansebooks.com**

THE

BIRTH OF JESUS.

BY

Rev. HENRY A. MILES, D. D.

AUTHOR OF "ORIGIN AND TRANSMISSION OF THE GOSPELS," "TRACES OF PICTURE-WRITING IN THE BIBLE."

"Beware lest any man spoil you through philosophy and vain deceit, after the tradition of men, after the rudiments of the world, and not after Christ."
St. Paul to the Colossians ii. 8

BOSTON:
LOCKWOOD, BROOKS, AND COMPANY.
381 WASHINGTON STREET.
1878.

CONTENTS.

		PAGE
Chapter I.	Introduction	5
II.	The Problem	19
III.	The Probable Facts	34
IV.	The Shepherds and the Magi	55
V.	After Theories	72
VI.	The Fight	95
VII.	The Fathers	125
VIII.	Patristic Reasoning	139
IX.	The Apostles' Creed	154
X.	Mariolatry	166
XI.	Conclusion	194

THE BIRTH OF JESUS.

CHAPTER I.

INTRODUCTION.

IT is the object of this book to examine those parts of the gospel narratives which relate to the birth of Jesus, in order to understand, if possible, what they intended to record.

A few words may explain the motives that lead to this investigation, and the spirit in which it is conducted.

If there be in the English language a monograph on this subject, it is not known to the writer of this book. Various commentaries on the Gospels offer brief explanations; but, perhaps, no critical reader has looked into them without disappointment. To discuss this point fully in such works would require disproportionate space, and it is generally dismissed in a few words.

The inquirer may next turn to Treatises on the Evidences of Christianity. In modern works of this kind the miraculous birth of Jesus is frequently not even alluded to. Scholars know what a prominent place this point held a few hundred years ago. The recent silence betrays doubts, and still further baffles the inquirer.

He finds a like silence on this subject in modern creeds. The ninth chapter of this book will describe the steps of the formation, in the fourth century, of what is commonly called *The Apostles' Creed*. Subsequent creeds often followed the style of that symbol of faith. But a marked change in their contents is now seen in nearly all Protestant creeds. The old clauses relating to the supernatural birth of Jesus are now omitted. The Christian consciousness of our age recognizes the difficulties and doubts connected with this subject, and makes concession to them. With good sense and propriety creeds are now usually limited to the expression, in some form, of a belief that Jesus was a divine manifestation in the flesh. Details are left to individual judgments, which, if they have ever carefully considered this subject, have doubtless reached diverse conclusions.

Two opposite poles of thought are sufficiently obvious. On the one hand is the lately proclaimed, but long believed, dogma of the " Immaculate Conception," which affirms that the Virgin Mary gave birth to God by the power of the Holy Ghost, without human intervention. On the other hand, to many minds there seems mingled with the records of the birth of Jesus such a mass of incredible interpretations that it has none of the aspects of a real event. The whole history is pushed aside with much the same feeling as is the fable of the birth of Minerva from the brain of Jupiter.

Between these extremes the minds of thoughtful teachers of religion often waver. Once in each year they read from the sacred desk the stories of the birth of Jesus, and can feel, as they think, a sincere faith in them. They are sustained by the hallowed memories that cluster around that season in which Jesus "came to visit us in great humility," and which, amid all the kindly feelings and beautiful customs of Christmas, draw every one into a believing mood. But even then, as we suppose, most ministers would prefer not to be questioned closely as to what the traditions relating to the first Christmas really mean.

We know that they would generally affirm that they believe exactly what the record says. But what the record says is still an open question; and if they reply that they take it in its obvious and literal sense, we suspect that few believe this with the same assured faith with which they believe other things.

Propositions of which we say that we believe them all equally, may have a very different hold upon the mind. There are other witnesses in the case than our affirmations. Probably no one reads ordinarily the story of the birth of Jesus in the same tone of voice with which he reads the Beatitudes. It seems impossible that these chapters should stand alike in our spiritual conviction. The preacher knows there are thoughtful and devout men among his hearers who look upon the account of that birth with bewildered and suspended minds. He would be glad to come into a truer relation to them; and they would be glad to see this subject in lights which would permit an untroubled belief.

Between a literal acceptance of the stories connected with our Lord's birth, and a rejection of them all as fables, critical literature has not yet furnished an accredited middle ground. Happily we are far removed from the ribald skepticism of the Deistical writers of the last century. Nothing is more reassuring than the freedom from sneering assaults from unbelievers, and the manly confidence in the truth among the friends of a sound Biblical criticism. Even those who shrink from a departure from traditional interpretations have little of the feeling of the Buddhist, who, regarding the destruction of any life as a sin, and seeing millions of animalculæ in a drop of water, at once destroyed the microscope that had made the unwelcome revelation.

Should a visitor from some other planet see in Roman Catholic countries the infant Jesus in his mother's arms, painted in millions of pictures, in churches, and on shrines and altars, and should he observe that prayers are offered to these a thousand fold more frequently than to any one else, would he not naturally conclude that the Christian's God is an infant, and that Christian adoration consists in the worship of a child?

How great would be his astonishment if he should contrast all this with the worship enjoined by Jesus, and with the prayers that have come down to us from the first century of the church.

It might be a long time before he could understand from what tone of mind arose this ascription of the godhead to a child. But his studies in history would at length suggest the true explanation. He would see that it was the influence of pagan literature which first invested that child with supernatural associations.

In the heathen mythologies it was believed that the gods often took human form. When in the fourth century a thin Christian varnish was given to the ancient paganism, parallelisms were eagerly sought between Jupiter and his offspring, and Jehovah and the Son of God. The life of Jesus was then written, once in Greek by lines taken entirely from Homer, and once in Latin by lines taken entirely from Virgil. These "Centons," as they were called, were famous books in their day. They are here referred to only as one token among numberless others of the drift of thought in the epoch when they appeared. That epoch originated the worship of a child, and made that child God.

At the Protestant Reformation the adoration of an infant was abandoned by the Reformers; but the theology on which that adoration rested was retained. This theology teaches that this infant, even before his birth, was the Almighty

God. "God of God" was laid in the manger of Bethlehem, and was carried in his mother's arms. Some think the Roman Catholic is more consistent with this theology than the Protestant. It seems strange that so little has been done to reform the theology on which this idolatry was engrafted. Why should we lay at the vestibule of Christianity an old heathen dogma, which, if made as prominent as formerly, would repel thousands, and is now repelling many, since it is in conflict with the criticism and thought of this age?

What if the records of the birth of Jesus have been misunderstood for hundreds of years? What if false opinions on this point have long been handed down from father to son? Do we not know that this has happened with many other dogmas? The more enlightened faith of our day protests against views of the *Atonement*, of *Total Depravity*, of *Future Punishment*, and of *Infant Damnation*, which have been believed for ages.

The old complaint that theology has not shared the progress of other sciences is at length losing its pertinency. Truth, which is in itself "the same yesterday, to-day, and forever," will necessarily assume different aspects according to the condition of our mental eyes. It would be evidence of imbecility or insanity to ask us to hold the astronomical views adopted before telescopes were invented.

"The whole scheme of Scripture," says one of the profoundest thinkers, "is not yet understood; and, if it ever comes to be understood, it must be in the same way as natural knowledge is come at; by the continuance and progress of learning and of liberty, and by particular persons attending to, comparing and pursuing intimations scattered up and down it, which are overlooked and disregarded by the generality of the world. Nor is it at all incredible that a book which has been so long in the possession of mankind should contain many truths as yet undiscovered."[1]

This is a sufficient answer to the sophistry in one of Lord Macaulay's Essays.[2] He contends that theology "is not a progressive science." A divine revelation makes all minds equal. A Newton, or a Locke, he says, can see no further than a Blackfoot Indian. This must be on the supposition that revelation is the only factor in

[1] Bishop Butler.
[2] See Macaulay's *Review of Ranke's History of the Popes.*

the case. Surely, our ability to comprehend revelation, to free it from traditional misrepresentations, and to clear our mental eye, is another factor. This necessitates a continued readjustment of old conclusions. The great historian was here advancing one of the brilliant paradoxes which at times fascinated his pen.

The limits of the change of opinion now advocated should be defined as well as its scope.

In undertaking to show that in the New Testament and the Primitive Church we are taught that Jesus was born in a natural generation, and was the son of Joseph as well as of Mary, nothing is said that is necessarily adverse to Arian or Trinitarian views of his personality. It is as conceivable on this hypothesis, as on any other, that a preëxisting angel, or the Deity himself, was incarnated in a body so generated. All our *a priori* speculations are out of place. We are interested to know what the Gospels *say*. Why for their teachings should we substitute the dogmatism of ignorant and misguided ages?

If it be asked why we care for one theory rather than the other, it seems a sufficient answer to point to the different effect upon our views of the reality of the person of Jesus. To how many minds he is not a real person! His existence seems to belong not to the domain of veritable history, but to that of legendary theology. Plato, Socrates, Cicero, Seneca, are real persons; but Jesus, to many, is a fabulous demi-god. His name stands for a spectre. The perplexing traditions of his birth cast a shadowy mystery over the whole of his life. Christians of all names do indeed say that they believe in his humanity; but to many this is little better than a mere make-belief. Is there any other name in history around which have gathered such a mass of confused and self-contradictory associations?

No sooner had the person of Jesus been enveloped in a mythical cloud than a host of perplexing questions arose to distract the Church. It was asked, Was his flesh of the same essence as his divinity? Was his body created or uncreated? If uncreated, did it once form a part of the Trinity? If created, when, where, and out of what, was it made? Was his body corruptible or incorruptible? If corruptible, how could it ascend to heaven? If incorruptible, how could he be said to have assumed human nature? If he was equal to the Father and the Spirit, why was he sent to suffer and die, rather than either of the other persons of the Trinity? Did he suffer in his human nature, or in his divine nature, or in both? If he suffered in his human nature alone, where is the infinite atonement? If he suffered in the divine nature, did the Father and the Spirit suffer with him? Did he have two wills, or only one will? How can a generated son be equal to an ungenerated father?

Every reader of ecclesiastical history knows that these are only a few of the problems that have fed the fires of controversy. Nor can it be denied that the generally accepted theology of to-day offers stumbling-blocks to faith. The distinction attempted to be drawn between what Jesus said in his human nature and what he said in his divine nature, implies prevarications which we should be slow to impute to a good man.

They thus interfere with the prompt movements of the heart. Not that there are no passionate expressions of love for Jesus; but have we ever tried to analyze the emotions probably at the bottom of them? We have, perhaps, found a sense of weakness, of a need of forgiveness and help, and a longing for peace and trust, all of which have looked out for an arm on which they may lean. But these emotions stand apart from any clear conception of him on whom it is said they rest. We mark their subjective intensity, and not their objective reality. Do those who are so absorbed in what they feel know how Jesus feels? Is it possible, with their dim views of his personality, to have a living sympathy with his soul?

Hence the frequent remark that the prevalent type of piety is wanting in manliness. If men feel that " Jesus has done all for them," that they have only to go to him " just as they are," that he " washes away their sins," and " hides them in the cleft of the rock," is it strange that this passive trust should lack an inward energy? Is not here one reason why so many keep on the same plane of Christian experience from the time of conversion to the time of death? This helpless reliance is thus regarded as the crowning work of him who came that they " might have life and might have it more abundantly." What we all need for our moral quickening is a profounder sympathy with the humanity of Jesus; but how can that sympathy exist under the shadows that cloud the scenes of his birth?

There are signs of the coming of a better day. The progress of our civilization is marked by a deeper appreciation of the character of Jesus — his gentleness, his disinterestedness, his self-sacrifice, the depth of his spiritual insight, the clearness and strength of his intellectual convictions, and the force of his will. These lead us into his soul. We see it was a human soul. Born into the world like man's soul, and like man's soul increasing in wisdom as he grew in stature, it was the vehicle of the spirit given to him " without measure," and coming upon him as he was fitted to receive it. By such a view he is not thrust out of the sphere of our human conceptions and of our intelligent love. Our faith may rest on more real and stable foundations.

Hence it does not seem too much to look for a deeper and sincerer manifestation of the spirit of Jesus when those mists of error are not interposed between him and our minds. That great soul, whose influence amid all these obstacles has weighed on the civilized world more than that of all other souls put together, may exert a renewed power when we can see him more clearly, and can love him more profoundly.

We have only glanced at some of the reasons which draw us to a subject that stands connected with many curious problems of Biblical criticism, with one of the most savage controversies that has disgraced the history of the Church, and with a wonderful literature, little known by Protestants, that grew out of the worship of the Virgin Mary.

We have no novel explanations to offer, but wish simply to " stand in the way and ask for the old paths."

It is only with a reverent hand that we presume to touch the sacred pictures which have been the world's delight and instruction through so many centuries; with the prayer, in the first place, that we may not mar their beauty, and, secondly, that if we fail to remove any of the blotches with which rude times have overlaid them, this success may be given to some other.

We write in the interest of no sect or creed, and we ask our readers to follow us in that candid and honest spirit by which we hope that we too may be guided.

CHAPTER II.

THE PROBLEM.

THERE are eight verses in the first chapter of the Gospel of St. Matthew, and thirteen verses in the first chapter of the Gospel of St. Luke, on which all the dogmas in regard to Christ's birth have been built.

It is so necessary for a just examination of our subject to have these verses readily under the eye, that we shall here quote the words of both Evangelists.

St. Matthew's Gospel reads as follows: —

CHAPTER i. 18. Now the birth of Jesus Christ was on this wise: When as his mother Mary was espoused to Joseph, before they came together, she was found with child of the Holy Ghost.

19. Then Joseph her husband, being a just man, and not willing to make her a public example, was minded to put her away privily.

20. But while he thought on these things, behold, the angel of the Lord appeared unto him in a

dream, saying, Joseph, thou son of David, fear not to take unto thee Mary thy wife: for that which is conceived in her is of the Holy Ghost;

21. And she shall bring forth a son, and thou shalt call his name Jesus; for he shall save his people from their sins.

22. Now all this was done that it might be fulfilled which was spoken of the Lord by the prophet, saying:

23. Behold, a virgin shall be with child, and shall bring forth a son, and they shall call his name Emmanuel, which being interpreted is, God with us.

24. Then Joseph, being raised from sleep did as the angel of the Lord had bidden him, and took unto him his wife:

25. And knew her not till she had brought forth her first-born son: and he called his name Jesus.

St. Luke's Gospel reads as follows: —

CHAPTER i. 26. And in the sixth month the angel Gabriel was sent from God unto a city of Galilee, named Nazareth,

27. To a virgin espoused to a man whose name was Joseph, of the house of David; and the virgin's name was Mary.

28. And the angel came in unto her and said, Hail, thou that art highly favored, the Lord is with thee: blessed art thou among women..

29. And when she saw him, she was troubled at his saying, and cast in her mind what manner of salutation this should be.
30. And the angel said unto her, Fear not Mary, for thou hast found favor with God.
31. And behold, thou shalt conceive in thy womb, and bring forth a son, and shalt call his name Jesus.
32. He shall be great, and shall be called the Son of the Highest; and the Lord God shall give unto him the throne of his father David:
33. And he shall reign over the house of Jacob for ever; and of his kingdom there shall be no end.
34. Then said Mary unto the angel, How shall this be, seeing I know not a man?
35. And the angel answered and said unto her, The Holy Ghost shall come upon thee, and the power of the Highest shall overshadow thee: therefore also that holy thing which shall be born of thee shall be called the Son of God.
36. And behold, thy cousin Elisabeth, she hath also conceived a son in her old age; and this is the sixth month with her who was called barren:
37. For with God nothing shall be impossible.
38. And Mary said, Behold the handmaid of the Lord, be it unto me according to thy word. And the angel departed from her.

Neither St. Mark nor St. John has one word relating to the details named in the above twenty-one verses. In the case of St. John an explanation has often been given of his silence. It is generally believed that he wrote after he had seen the other three Gospels; and it may not have fallen into his design, it has been said, to repeat what he had there found correctly narrated.

But his design, whatever it was, did not prevent him from repeating many other things which his predecessors had recorded; why did he omit this? As he wrote, he says, John xx. 31, to show "that Jesus is the Christ, the Son of God," it is not easy to see why there is no reference to such proofs as the above texts are now thought to furnish, especially as he must have known that his work might fall into hands that would never receive the other Gospels.

It is even more difficult to account for the silence of St. Mark, who was a companion of St. Peter, from whose lips, as is believed, he obtained the materials of his Gospel. St. Peter was a native of Galilee, was one of the most intimate disciples of Jesus, and doubtless personally knew his parents. These marvelous incidents that preceded the birth of his Master, if they occurred in the manner in which in later times they have been understood, must have been the subject of frequent conversation in the circle in which he lived, and must have been impressed deeply upon his ardent mind. How happens it that we do not get one word about them through his interpreter, St. Mark?

There is another question somewhat perplexing. St. Matthew's eight verses give account of the angelic visitation to Joseph, but have nothing to say in regard to the revelation made to Mary. The fact is precisely opposite in the thirteen verses in St. Luke, where we read of the angelic visitation to Mary, but nothing is said of the revelation made to Joseph. Of course, in such brief memoirs some things must have been omitted by each writer, and we have no full history until we put all their accounts together; but there does not seem to be a ready answer to the question, why, if they attached importance to these traditions, each writer gave only half of the story, not knowing that anybody would report the other half.

There are still other queries that must have suggested themselves to every thoughtful reader.

If our common interpretation of the above verses be correct, how happened it that John the Baptist was so ignorant of Jesus? Twice he said, "I knew him not." John i. 31, 33. They were nearly of the same age, had been brought up in the same region, their mothers were cousins, and were well acquainted with each other, and, according to the received interpretation, both mothers had the most amazing angelic visitations, in regard to which they conversed together.

Christian art has interpreted all these facts as implying a familiar acquaintance with each other, and a mutual acquaintance on the part of their children. In numberless "Holy Families," the infant John and the infant Jesus are represented as saluting each other. It is true the children may have grown up apart; but even then, on the supposition of a literal understanding of the above texts, it seems incomprehensible that these stupenduous events attending the birth of these children, events which must have been in their families the subject of frequent conversation and auguries, should not have led John to know Jesus.

Our wonder does not here cease. Did not Jesus himself know of the marvelous circumstances that preceded his birth? Did not his mother, who "kept all these sayings in her heart," ever speak of them to that child in regard to whom they had excited such surprising expectations? How happens it, then, that Jesus never referred to them when he was so often intent upon proving that he came from God?

It can hardly be maintained that some general words of his, such as, " I came down from Heaven," " I am from above," " whom the Father sent into the world," are such decisive references to his birth, as, in the case supposed, we should expect from his lips. Phrases of an equivalent meaning he applied to his disciples, whom, he said, he sent into the world, as the Father had sent him. Had it been a point capable of proof, or one of admitted belief in the circle of his family and friends, that his origin was generically different from any other being, that his birth had been foretold by celestial visitants, and that he had been supernaturally conceived, does it not seem amazing that Jesus never once clearly appealed to this evidence of his divine mission?

When he was arraigned as a common disturber of the peace, Pilate wanted to know who he was, and showed signs of a willingness to release him.

Jesus said, "For this was I born, and for this cause came I into the world, that I might bear witness to the truth." John xviii. 37. Was not here one place where we should have expected him to give some hint of the miraculous manner of his birth? If this had been a point that was then believed, or was capable of proof, could anything have been more in his defence? Why was not some reference to it here made?

Nor is this all. Why is it that throughout the Gospels there is no appeal to the events above recited? Excepting in the verses quoted, those events are as much ignored in all the Gospels, and in every part of each Gospel, as if they had been recorded in another history, and concerned some other being.

If it should be said that St. John refers to them in the Proem of his Gospel, when he says, "The Word was God . . . . and the Word became flesh," we must ask the reader to pause for one moment upon the meaning of that statement. It is possible to thrust interpretations into it that go a great way beyond what it affirms. It does not say where, or how, or when the Divine Spirit was incarnated in Jesus Christ. It does not, therefore, conflict with the supposition that God's spirit came upon him gradually as he "increased in wisdom and stature," and came in harmony with the development of his mental and moral life. Thus these words seem to us to have no necessary bearing upon the question of a miraculous birth.

If it should be said that this Proem of St. John's Gospel affirms a *personal* existence of Jesus, before his birth on earth, it may be well to ask, not only if we do not assign to the Evangelist's words ideas which are not necessarily there, but also if we do not impute to him the very doctrine which he undertook to refute. It was against a Gnostic conception of some Eon, or Being, distinct from God, that St. John's introduction is generally supposed to be aimed; and he says that it was God's Logos that was in the beginning, which created the world, and became incarnated; and this he repeatedly affirms was no distinct person, but was God himself, as God's Life and Light were God himself.

Perhaps it will be said that in such brief memoirs one statement of a miraculous birth was enough. But how did each writer know that it had been stated at all? Besides, as a matter of fact, each writer often repeated what the others had said. Nor this alone. Each at times repeated what he himself had recorded. The feeding of the five thousand, the predictions of Christ's sufferings, of his rejection by the Jews, of his crucifixion by the priests, these, and other important events in their narratives, were not dismissed once for all. They were referred to again and again. Now the events preceding Christ's birth, taking them as generally understood, are not only among the most extraordinary in the Evangelical Narratives, but are the most important in their bearing upon the great point which the Gospels were written to establish. Why this silence about them?

Our surprise culminates in considering one other fact. We have in the Book of Acts reports of sermons preached by the Apostles who endeavored to prove that Jesus is the Son of God; and following the Book of Acts, we have Epistles sent to churches in different parts of the world, designed to set forth the same leading truth. But in all of them, Sermons and Epistles, there is no statement of the miraculous conception of Christ.

Take the sermon recorded in the third chapter of Acts, which Peter preached after he had healed the lame man at the Beautiful Gate of the Temple. His object was to explain to the Jews who Christ was, as one glorified by the God of Abraham, Isaac, and Jacob, but denied by them, and killed, and raised from the dead. How pertinent to his purpose to refer to his supernatural birth, if that had been a point capable of proof or belief.

Or take the sermon, recorded in the seventh chapter of Acts, which Stephen preached just before his martyrdom, — the longest apostolical sermon of which we have any record, — giving a *résumé* of Jewish and Christian history, from the call of Abraham to the crucifixion of Jesus. Why not one hint about this miraculous conception?

Look, also, to the sermon which Paul preached in Antioch of Pisidia, recorded in the thirteenth chapter of Acts, a sermon recounting prominent events from the exodus out of Egypt to the resurrection of Jesus. Why not one word said about his supernatural birth?

Moreover, in the Epistles of St. Paul, of St. Peter, of St. John, there is no distinct allusion to this point, though, had it been then understood as it is understood now, there could have been nothing more natural, or more decisive than to adduce it.

It is true, some have quoted the expressions of St. Paul, Romans ix. 5, "of whom as concerning the flesh Christ came;" implying, it may be thought, that he had also another origin. But the original expression, κατὰ σάρκα, means, as the commentators tell us, hereditary descent, and so damages the use often made of the text.

Another expression, Philippians ii. 6, "Who, being in the form of God — took upon him the form of a servant;" has, as it may be said, a reference to a supernatural origin. But perhaps we shall by and by see that later opinions ascribed a meaning to these words which the writer could not have had in his mind. And, moreover, in regard to that something which Christ had in him higher than what he inherited by natural descent, that something which made him in the form of God, — as that might have come upon him at any period of his growth, — what proof have these texts of a miraculous birth?

In regard to the Epistles, it must be remembered that they were sent to the churches before the Gospels had been written. At least, we have no distinct traces of the Gospels until after the transmission of the Epistles. Every reader will at once see what bearing this fact has upon the argument before us.

It might be now said that the writers of the Epistles felt that there was no need of relating the miraculous birth of Jesus, or of appealing to this as a proof of his divine origin, if they knew that the history of that birth was already in the hands of their readers. But there is absolutely nothing to show that the Romans, the Corinthians, the Galatians, the Ephesians, the Thessalonians, had any knowledge of that history, had ever heard of it, or had the least suspicion of it.

Indeed, the presumption is all the other way. The family traditions were appended to the memoirs of Jesus at a later time. They occupied no place in the first, the Epistolary, publication of the Gospel. Hence they were the groundwork of no argument, and received no distinct allusion. It seems incredible that Paul and Peter and John regarded them as of importance in the life of Jesus.

Certainly, here are noteworthy facts. This uniform, persistent, and unbroken reticence is in strange contrast with what we find at a later day. A way of referring to the birth of Jesus sprung up in after ages which ascribed an importance to the eight verses of St. Matthew, and to the thirteen verses of St. Luke, which, so far as appears, was never imagined by Jesus and his apostles. History tell us when it sprung up, and where it sprung up, and how it sprung up, and how it colored the whole stream of Christian thought from that time onwards, and shapes opinions even to this day.

And history tells us, also, of the wild hypotheses which, in modern times, have been invented to get rid of these interpretations. Without referring to the English Deists of the last century, who ridiculed the stories of Christ's birth as absurd fables, we need only allude to Strauss, who sets them all aside as myths, that is, as something which was " characterized by the rich pictorial and imaginative mode of thought and expression of primitive ages."

Professor Weisse maintained that these narratives were pious imitations of Grecian legends, designed to show that Christ had an origin something like that of heathen gods; and of this hypothesis Neander well says that " Weisse has transferred his own mode of contemplating heathen myths to a people that would have revolted from it."

THE PROBLEM.

Eichhorn regarded these stories as the expressions of an unscientific age, addicted to wonder, and in love with the marvelous. Paulus distinguished between fact and opinion, and held that this last covered the record with the drapery of miracle, which must be drawn aside to see the historical verity. Kant held to a moral interpretation, looking for a sense which agrees with the laws of the pure reason, and he regarded the miraculous stories only as an imaginative description of an ideal humanity pleasing to God. De Wette thought that after Jesus had become famous, reports about him were repeated from mouth to mouth, till his early years became gradually encircled with these poetical embellishments. Renan believes that these tales are legendary accounts, framed after the pattern of similar stories in the Old Testament.

In view of this wide diversity of opinion it may be well, first of all, to consider carefully what the gospel record actually says. And what if we find that the difficulty of explanation lies less in that than in ourselves? If we see that the record is right, and that it is we who are wrong, we who have blundered over it, this will be a kind of discovery which has often been made before.

CHAPTER III.

THE PROBABLE FACTS.

TO the mere English reader each Gospel seems to be entirely the composition of the writer whose name it bears; and we usually regard it as a connected work from one and the same hand. An acquaintance with the original language shows that this impression is incorrect. Criticism soon learns to disintegrate each Gospel, and to recognize in the different style of different portions different documents which had been put together.

An illustration may give some light to this subject. We may suppose an incident in the life of Washington to have been described in the rude diction of a common soldier, writing at the time of its occurrence, and afterwards other facts of the same incident to have been described in the plain historical language of Mr. Sparks, and more ornately in the flowing periods of Mr. Everett. Bancroft may have put all the accounts together just as he found them, and the whole may be known as his history.

Now if that history should be translated into French, and from that into Spanish, and from that into Italian, these peculiarities of diction would be likely to be worn away in passing through so many hands; and to the Italian reader the work might seem homogeneous, and all from the pen of Bancroft.

But suppose the Italian reader should be well acquainted with English, and should read the history, not after these successive translations, but just as Bancroft left it; he would at once mark the diversity of style, and would unhesitatingly assign portions of the narrative to the unlettered soldier above referred to, and portions to the chaste words of Sparks, and other portions to the rounded periods of Everett, and connecting portions to the historian Bancroft. If he were a master of the English tongue, and acquainted with the different styles of these writers, he never would make the blunder of assigning all these different compositions to one and the same hand.

In each Gospel, not as we have it after numberless translations into other languages, but as we find it in the original tongue, there is a variety of style somewhat corresponding to the above supposition. For example, the first four verses of Luke's Gospel are in pure Greek, and then follows an entirely different diction full of Hebraisms. It is the account of the birth of John and of Jesus; and if the reader will notice the fifth verse of the first chapter he will see that it begins as a separate and distinct document.

A similar remark may be made of the first chapter of Matthew. The first seventeen verses appear as an independent genealogy. Accordingly they are called "The Book of the Generation of Jesus Christ." Then the eighteenth verse begins as a separate record, though the difference in style between this and the rest of Matthew's Gospel is not so marked as in the case of Luke, for Luke was a man of more culture than Matthew.

The poetical rhythm of the *Magnificat*, Luke i. 46–55, and of the *Benedictus Dominus* of Zacharias, Luke i. 68–79, is wholly different from the general, matter-of-fact style of Luke. The last chapter of Mark critics believe to be an appendix to that Gospel. John's Gospel they suppose originally ended with the last verse of the twentieth chapter. The first part of the eighth chapter of John, it is thought, is misplaced, and the twenty-second chapter of Luke has some peculiarities of diction that distinguish it from the rest of that book. His genealogy, Luke iii. 23–38, he probably quoted from some family record, without once dreaming of indorsing its entire literal accuracy.

At the time the Gospels were composed there were many memoirs of the birth and life of Jesus in circulation. Luke expressly bears witness to this fact. He begins his record with the words, "Forasmuch as many have taken in hand to set forth in order a declaration of those things which are most surely believed among us." So also the existence of apocryphal Gospels is attested by ecclesiastical history. It is probable that a vast number of these memoirs had been written for the use of different churches; some containing the recollections of one apostle, some those of another, some the reminiscences in the family of Jesus, or brief annals by various hands of what he said and did in the places he visited. Several of these documents were put together; and the four collections most generally approved have come down to us under the four names they bear.

We must not suppose, therefore, that Mary

improvised the *Magnificat* at the time of the visitation, or that Zacharias sang the *Benedictus* at the birth of his son. These were probably composed long afterwards, as expressive of the supposed feelings at the time, and were inserted in the family memoirs to which the subsequent eminence of John and of Jesus gave rise.

These family memoirs, as Olshausen suggests, were adopted by Luke; oftentimes, as that critic adds, " quite unchanged or but slightly amended." And so it happened that more or less of them were attached to the evangelical narrative, none, indeed, to Mark, or John, a few only to Matthew, but more to Luke.

Apparently, as we judge such things, they were accidentally attached, as it is evident the apostles did not assign much importance to these domestic reminiscences. Of this we have proof in the little use they made of them, as we have seen in the preceding chapter. We shall find a still further proof when we come to mark what these reminiscences really mean.

An angel appeared to Zacharias announcing the birth of John. An angel appeared to Mary announcing the birth of Jesus. An angel appeared to Joseph to allay his suspicions, and to suggest the flight into Egypt. What was the origin of this language about angels, and what does it denote?

These questions carry us back to the early literary culture of the Hebrew people. Prior to alphabetic writing they undoubtedly followed the fashion of all other nations in the use of picture-language. Some visible representation stood for every mental experience.

How do thoughts come into the mind? How do hopes and persuasions enter the heart? To primitive people it did not seem that these are the natural effect of our own reflections, as indeed they may not always be. It was believed that all deep impressions were sent within us directly by God. If sent, it was supposed there was a messenger to bear them. Hence sprung up the idea of a multitude of celestial beings charged with the duty of bringing convictions and emotions to human souls.

Early art, prior to the invention of letters, expressed this belief, as we have said, by pictures, which in turn helped to fasten it more firmly on the popular mind. The messenger was depicted as being in youthful beauty, aerial and winged; and names, found during the Babylonian captivity, were given to the chief actors in this imaginary host. Before the use of verbal language, how else could there be expressions of feelings and thoughts supposed to have come from heaven? These pictures of angels, and the language which subsequently grew out of them, were a necessity in the course of human progress.

Thus, in our abstract terms, we say, "I am convinced of such a truth." But in early ages men did not regard this conviction as something evolved by themselves. They thought that God sent it to them, and that an angel brought it. Men continued to use this picturesque diction after it had passed out of its first literal signification. Indeed, it retains to some extent its hold upon the imagination to this day. We still say the thought came to me *like an angel from heaven*. We say also that we are sustained by *the angel of hope*.

When we ourselves use this metaphorical language, we see at once that it is employed in a secondary sense. But we do not always remember that the writers of the New Testament may have so used it also. To their words we ascribe a bald, literal meaning; and so we make the mistake which, a thousand years hence, an interpreter of words used now may make, who, when he reads that we were *thunderstruck* at hearing some news, should gravely say that we had actually received a shock of an electrical bolt.

In the mouths of the evangelical writers this language about angels was probably thus used in a subjective sense. It was employed to carry on, in the form of a dialogue with a supposed outward person, a wholly internal process of thought. Unlettered persons among us still use language in a similar way. A plain man described his doubts about helping a beggar in the following style: "Sympathy for the poor fellow said give; but justice urged that the beggar was able to work." This is exactly in the manner of the verses in St. Matthew and St. Luke, only the writers of these verses would have called sympathy and justice by the name of angels. Until we see what the sacred writers really intended by this phraseology, we turn all their artless stories into an absurd travesty.

Evil spirits also, as it was believed, had a mission to bring wicked suggestions and wishes; hence the whole hierarchy of demons. The temptation of Jesus is, as we suppose, usually interpreted as an internal experience, and not as an outward scene. It may be added that Jewish scholars, who know the meaning of old Hebrew modes of expression, do not believe that a person is implied by the word angel. (See Neander, vol. i. p. 42.)

In the tenth and eleventh chapters of the Acts we see a frequent angelophania, or appearance of angels. But this was not appealed to in early times as evidence of the truth of Christianity. It was understood to be the way in which illiterate men expressed themselves. This mode of speech, as we have said, belongs everywhere to certain stages of culture, in which men make no discrimination between the operations of their own minds and the influence of higher powers. All that they think and feel in reflective states they regard as coming to them from above. Thus, in the Greek mythology, the warlike were actuated by Mars, the skilled by Apollo, the loving by Venus, the wise by Zeus; and Socrates explained how the functions of these divinities ceased as soon as abstract terms were invented.

So was it in the case of the Hebrews. The use of abstract terms superseded the angelophania; or at least banished it to the realm of poetry, in which, as we have before remarked, it still survives.¹

Zacharias, a priest, married (for in those days marriage was a holy state, and it was impious to suppose that one contracted impurity thereby), shared the feeling so general in his day that the happiest lot of man was found in the parental relation; and he and his wife had prayed for this blessing, which, through their age, had now seemed hopeless. Burning incense in a dark inclosure,² lighted only by flames fitfully playing on the ascending smoke, his eye rested on some convolution at the right hand of the altar, as he was revolving in his mind his life-long prayer; and a persuasion took possession of his soul that, after all, God would answer it.

---

¹ Some attempt to explain the pictorial formation of Hebrew phrases may be found in a work published in Boston by Little, Brown, & Co., entitled *Traces of Picture-writing in the Bible*, by the author of this book.

² "A sacred chamber into which the light of day never penetrated, but where the dim fires of the altar, and the chandeliers, which were never extinguished, gave a solemn and uncertain light, still more bedimmed by the clouds of smoke arising from the newly-fed altar of incense." Milman's *History of Christianity*, chapter 2.

Grotius thought that Zacharias offered up the national prayer for the coming of the Messiah, and that the expression, *thy prayer is heard*, refers to this.

How often, in human experience, vivid subjective states mingle with outward objects, so that they mutually recall each other! Who can say there was nothing divine in his persuasion, or that there was nothing unusual in the bestowment of a child to their advanced years? If we do not recognize something "supernatural" here, as certain metaphysical disquisitions explain that word, does it follow that God was not in all this? It was at least natural that, afterwards, the grateful and gratified father should devoutly recall the alternate hopes and fears that marked that memorable moment of self-communion.

To the incense-burning priest it seemed as if his backwardness to believe in the possibility of the coveted blessing was a sinful distrust of the divine power, and must be punished by a silence enjoined by the same angel-persuasion [1] that now had influence over him. Examples of self-imposed silence have not been unknown. See Daniel x. 15. We find them in almost every age, and in some cases men, as a voluntary penance,

[1] "Μη δυναμενος λαλησαι dicitur is, qui vel propter physica, vel propter moralia impedimenta loqui non potest." Rosenmüller, *in loco.*

THE PROBABLE FACTS. 45

have not spoken a word for fifteen or twenty years.

The distrust and self-punishment of Zacharias were recalled years afterwards, when the eminence of the child had given such importance to these reminiscences. If they had been recorded in some family memoirs, and formed an episode in the private life of this domestic circle, they might easily get attached to the Gospel of Luke, though of no importance whatever as any historical proof.

The universal belief that the long-expected Messiah was soon to appear led every mother to ask, "Who knows but that my child may be the favored one of God?" A young woman, named Mary, had been espoused, at the age of sixteen, as the legends of the Church say, to a man much older than herself, by the name of Joseph, whose business it was, as Justin Martyr records, to make yokes and ploughs.

In those days espousal was in fact a marriage. It gave the rights of a husband. Separation could be effected only by a bill of divorce. Thus the law recognized this as a legal wedlock. But though the parties were really husband and wife, they did not live together until after some public ceremony of marriage. The phrase that described their state before this ceremony is, πρὶν ἢ συνελθεῖν, that is, before they lived together (see Matthew i. 18), it being the same phrase found in Acts i. 6, where we read, when the disciples *came together*, and in many other Biblical texts. It is true, however, that it sometimes has the secondary meaning of cohabitation, though this is not its uniform signification.

But it may be asked, Did not Mary say distinctly, in Luke i. 34, "I know not a man"? The student of the original Greek knows that the word here translated man is ἄνδρα, the usual New Testament word for husband. She only denied that she had a publicly recognized husband. Accordingly Olshausen translates the sentence, "I do not live in a marriage connection with any one."

At her age Mary was called a virgin, παρθένος. The exclusive meaning now generally attached to that word is modern. *Virgin* is the translation of the Hebrew word עַלְמָה, which means of *marriageable age*. (See Gesenius' Hebrew Lexicon.) Thus a virgin could be a mother. We are told in Isaiah vii. 14, that a virgin shall be a

THE PROBABLE FACTS.   47

mother.¹ To express our modern idea of virginity, other phrases were used, as may be seen

¹ If we accept the common interpretation of the birth of Jesus, and follow literally the words of Scripture, the birth referred to in Isaiah vii. 14, was just as supernatural and miraculous as that of Christ, and all the wonderful speculations gathered around the latter may as reasonably cluster around the former. We do not forget the explanation usually resorted to, that what was foretold in the time of Ahaz had its fulfillment at the time of Christ. But in regard to this we quote the sensible words of Olshausen: "The immediate grammatical sense of the passage, Isaiah vii. 14, necessarily requires a reference to something present, since the παρθένος who was to bring forth Immanuel, is represented by the prophet as a *sign to Ahaz*. A reference to the Messiah born of a virgin centuries afterwards, appears to answer no end whatever for the immediate circumstances. It is most natural to suppose that by παρθένος is meant the betrothed of the prophet called in Isaiah viii. 3, נְבִיאָה, as being his wife. Παρθένος, equivalent to עַלְמָה, a young woman, is indeed in itself different from בְּתוּלָה which necessarily denotes pure virginity. Looking at the passage free from prejudice, one is necessarily led to expect that Ahaz must have had something given him which *he* would live to see. It is very forced to refer the period of two or three years spoken of, to the coming of the Messiah, born centuries after." If one asks, what was there wonderful, what was there worthy to be called a "sign," in a young woman's bringing forth a child, we find an answer to this question in Olshausen, who says that "the unity of reference lies in the name Immanuel;" and if we ask further, why did St. Matthew refer to this passage in Isaiah, we probably find the reason in the fact that something took place which could be

in Judges xxi. 12, Genesis xxiv. 16. So also in the writings of the Fathers, not indeed uniformly, but frequently, those women are called virgins to whom, in its modern sense, that word could not be applied.[1]

Who can paint the tender, prophetic thoughts which that young mother hardly dared whisper to herself? Only those can do it who can recall the emotions of the first consciousness of mater-

described in those old prophetic words, for now a young woman brought forth a child who was, in a sense higher even than in the time of Ahaz, a revealer of God, that is, an Immanuel. In regard to the sense of the παρθένος it may be added that the Fathers often interpret it as equivalent to our English word *bride*. This is the sense the word must have in Isaiah xlvii. 1. So in Esther ii. 19, we see that the king's concubines are called *virgins*. In Joel i. 8, we read that a virgin mourns the death of her husband.

[1] Tertullian, in the first half of the third century, applied the word *virgins* to those who lived in unlawful cohabitation with men. In the sermons of St. John Chrysostom, the mulieres subintroductæ are called *virgins*. In the letters of St. Jerome, young women who led criminal lives are called *virgins*. In the *Letters of St. Leo*, pope from 440 to 460, young married women are called *virgins*. In all these cases one sense of this word was followed which had been established for more than a thousand years, for Homer calls a mother of two brave sons a "virgin." *Iliad*, lib. ii. line 514; and Herodotus speaks of certain "virgins" who presented their thank-offering for safe delivery in childbirth. Book iv. chap. 34.

nity. Was Mary to be a mother? But she said to herself, ἄνδρα οὐ γινώσκω, which Olshausen translates, "I do not live in a marriage connection;" and therefore it is too soon to open my heart to that great hope. And yet, who knows but that God has already in my virtual wedlock favored me, that his protecting providence will shelter me, and that even I may be the chosen one to give his Messiah to the world, so that to my son may be applied the words recorded in Psalm lxxxix. 4; Isaiah ix. 7, and Jeremiah xxxiii. 15?[1]

In after years how distinctly she recalled the anxious mental debates of the first consciousness of her maternity, she who from her espousal lived in holy wedlock, and knew not one of those associations of impurity which the grossness of aftertimes ascribed to that state; she who set forth in her own simple and primitive style the

[1] The fact that the words put into the mouth of the angel who addressed Mary were made up of quotations from the passages above referred to, seems a further indication that these words were not uttered by a celestial personage, in our modern sense of that word; though one commentator suggests that he sees no difficulty in the idea that angels may quote the Old Testament, and carefully read the Bible "to learn the gracious dispensations of God."

dialogue she carried on with herself, representing every good persuasion as an angel coming from the very chief places of heaven,[1] and weaving finally her joy into song, the whole composing a beautiful family memoir, which St. Luke had procured somewhere, and has handed down to us as a sweet and touching picture, though it was never thought of as any documentary proof until subsequent ages had misinterpreted and misused it.

Joseph, too, was not expecting that his wife would so soon become a mother. In her modesty, and in a reserve perhaps the greater for their disparity of years, she did not speak to him of her condition; time would reveal it. Accordingly the expression in this artless history is εὑρέθη. She was found in that state perhaps on some return after a few weeks' absence, for in these prim-

---

[1] This conception of some angels as coming from before the face of God is Persian. The *Zendavesta* refers to seven spirits who stand nearest the throne. After the Babylonian captivity the notion found its way into currents of Jewish thought. Allusion is made to it in various parts of the Old Testament written under Chaldean influence. See Zechariah vi. 5. But the idea nowhere appears prior to the time of that influence. Probably it came at length to denote those impressions which were most surely divine.

itive times business like Joseph's was not stationary, but was carried on from place to place.

How great was his surprise and joy! In after life he well remembered the thoughts he had then revolved. It had seemed too great a blessing to come to him. He had dwelt on that idea so much that he had even supposed it possible, that Mary had been unfaithful to him! Who can describe the mingled pathos and humor with which the old man used to tell the story, the smiles of surprise, and the tears of gratitude, that alternated in those earliest remembrances of that holy child.

Does a father's heart find any difficulty in interpreting this history, if he will not overlay it with prodigies that take it out of the sphere of all human experience, and will recognize here the action of that one dear nature which is common to us all? And so Joseph used to describe his foolish suspicions, and to tell how they were all allayed by the angel conviction that God's good providence was in all this, and would make his son a light and blessing to the world.

And then, afterwards, the thought came to him in the night, in view of the dangers that beset the life of his child, that he must go where the hand of power could not harm it. We are told that he was warned *in a dream.* But it is by no means necessary to suppose that this was an impression made upon his passive mind when his senses were locked in slumber.

The word *dream* in the Hebrew language covers all deep impressions in quiet and reflective hours. Joseph had heard much of the character of Herod. It made him anxious. He felt that there was but one way of safety, and that was flight. That was borne clear and strong upon his mind, as an inspiration from God, a vision from heaven, as it may have been, and was not the less likely to have been because it came to him when his senses were awake. And here was another of those reminiscences of the birth and early life of Jesus, which fond parents loved to recall, and were fittingly treasured as family traditions, though constituting no important evidence of the divine mission of their son.

Their son, we repeat. The son of Joseph as well as of Mary. So Jesus was regarded during his life. The pedigree of Joseph derived all its importance from the fact that he was the father of Jesus. Jesus was called his son in the common speech of his day. "Is not this the carpenter's son? Is not his mother called Mary?" Matthew xiii. 55. "And they said, Is not this Joseph's son?" Luke iv. 22. "And they said, Is not this Jesus, the son of Joseph, whose father and mother we know?" John vi. 42. "Philip findeth Nathanael and saith unto him, We have found him of whom Moses in the law, and the prophets, did write, Jesus of Nazareth, the son of Joseph." John i. 45.

Surely Mary, the mother, ought to be regarded as a competent witness in the case, and she said to her son, when she found him sitting with the doctors in the Temple, "Son, why hast thou thus dealt with us? behold thy father and I have sought thee sorrowing." Luke ii. 48.

And now, in surveying the exegesis offered in this chapter, as also that submitted in the chapter following, no doubt every reader may suggest other interpretations which, without the supposition of a miracle, will account for all the facts recorded in the texts under review. It is an important consideration that so many explanations *may* be suggested. The greater the number of possible hypotheses the greater the incredibility of the astounding traditions of past ignorant ages.

Subsequent pages will show how absolutely unfounded these traditions are. But before the evidence of this is submitted, our attention may be given to other incidents, connected with the birth of Jesus, in regard to which the imagination has run wild. We refer to the stories of the shepherds and the Magi.

CHAPTER IV.

THE SHEPHERDS AND THE MAGI.

THE rejoicing of the shepherds that watched their flocks by night, and the visit of the Magi, are two other beautiful events connected with the birth of Jesus, and we will now try to understand what they were.

We must, for the moment, lay aside a thousand poetic associations that have been attached to them, for such associations have been the growth of subsequent ages, — the expressions of grateful and devout hearts, delighted here to find what is wonderful, and pleased just in proportion as the subject is lifted up into regions of awe and poetic significance.

No words can be necessary to show that these incidents, whatever they were, produced but little impression at the time. We find the account of the shepherds only in the Gospel of St. Luke, and throughout the sacred canon there is not a hint of it, in sermon, or letter, or narrative, by any one else. St. Luke probably found the story in some domestic memoirs or tradition of the family of Mary, and appended it to his history.

Even in the family of Mary, as is evident, the story left no abiding impression. St. John tells us that the members of that family once besought Jesus to manifest himself openly to the world, and he adds, "For neither did his brethren believe in him." John vii. 5. At another time, as St. Mark says, his friends laid hold of him, "for they said, He is beside himself." Mark iii. 21. How could such things have been had the story of the shepherds and of the Magi left any deep mark in the memory of his family?

Probably then, in some incidental and almost unnoticed occurrence, we shall find the true origin of these narratives,—some little by-act which perhaps Mary alone laid up in her heart, with no thought that it would be the tiny seed of a tree whose leaves would spread over the whole earth.

In naming a possible explanation, one exposes himself to the derision of many whose minds have long been settled on other conclusions which they do not wish to have disturbed. The new suggestion has a show of presumption in the outset, as if it could weigh anything with the opinions of all the world in the other scale. But fair-minded readers will cover an honest inquiry with no such odium. Rather will they consider with candor an investigation which tries to go beneath unreasoning and hazy traditions, and to find something consistent with the admitted facts of the case.

Much that is said about poor, humble, simple-hearted shepherds comes from modern life. Shepherds near Bethlehem, eighteen centuries ago, were not what shepherds are now. The care of their flocks was the business of the wealthiest and most intelligent men. They were generally devout men, for such was the common type of the Hebrew character; and if Bethlehem was regarded as the predicted birthplace of the expected Messiah, the shepherds of that neighborhood might hear with wonder and joy of the birth of every infant on whom their great hope could possibly rest.

Joseph and Mary may have arrived at the home of some men who divided their time between that home in Bethlehem, and the care of their flocks by night on the neighboring hills. The utmost uncertainty exists, as everybody knows, in regard to the precise spot where Jesus was born. Some think it was a cave or grotto where cattle were kept, and both Justin Martyr and Origen say that this was the uninterrupted tradition of Bethlehem; while others believe that the birth took place in the lower part of a building used as a stable, while the upper stories were for human habitation, the domestic arrangement so common in the East.

All this is simply conjecture. It is of more importance to observe that the owners of the premises which Joseph and Mary occupied may have been their friends. There is an old church tradition that Andrew was one of the shepherds, and that afterwards, in his old age, he became one of the twelve. It may have been with him that Joseph and Mary stayed. What more natural than that her youth, and a beauty, the traditions of which have been so long preserved, should awaken the liveliest interest in all hearts?

We have not been told how long Mary had been in Bethlehem before the birth of her child; but when the joyful event took place, and her friends on the hillsides were informed of it by some messenger, coming to them with torches, and reporting the birth of a son, in the favored line of David. who possibly might fulfill their hopes, and telling them that if they would go into the town they might see the new-born in its lowly abode, how natural that these shepherds should rejoice, and it should seem to them as if the stars of heaven were shouting sweet words of peace and good will! Have there been no times in our life when we felt as if a thousand voices, all around, syllabled the deep emotions of our heart? On entering Bethlehem they may have spoken of their feelings to the delighted mother, who, as we read, "kept all these things and pondered them in her heart;" though such relations would not have a like interest to anybody else.

Neander and Schleiermacher are of opinion that this little episode about the shepherds was some detached memoir, made probably by the shepherds themselves. Neander says: "The facts may be supposed to have been as follows: in after times the faithful were anxious to preserve the minute features of the life of Jesus. We see every day how anxiously men look for individual traits in the childhood of great men. Especially would any one who had opportunity prosecute such researches in the remarkable place where

Christ was born. Perhaps one of these inquirers there found one of the shepherds who had witnessed these events, and whose memory of them was vividly recalled after his conversion to Christianity. We cannot be sure that such a man would give, with literal accuracy, the words that he had heard." [1]

If we suppose that here was substantially the whole occurrence, it would be in accordance with the then style of expression with unlettered Hebrews, to narrate it as we find it in the Gospel of Luke. If we see an air of naturalness and truthfulness in this narrative, as thus explained, if it seems that the common, the universal feelings of human hearts here display themselves, perhaps we shall feel a confidence in the truth of this history which we cannot have in the prodigies with which subsequent ages have overlaid it.

The story of the Magi is found nowhere except in the second chapter of the Gospel of St. Matthew, nor is there the least allusion to it in any other place in the New Testament. How fruitful it has been of wonderful legends and fanciful speculations in all past ages! Before sci-

[1] Neander's *Life of Christ*, Harper's edit., p. 22.

ence had revealed to the world what a star is in our solar system, popular credulity saw no difficulty in believing that one of the planets of the firmament moved along just above the heads of these men from the East, and stood over the house where the infant Jesus was laid. In a vast number of old church pictures all this is edifyingly represented.

But after a while even this needed some additional element of wonder; and so Ignatius, in one of his epistles says, "This star sparkled brilliantly beyond all other stars, while the other stars with the sun and moon formed a choir around it, but its blaze outshone them all."

Commentators in recent times, seeing the absurdity of this, have contented themselves in saying with Schleiermacher, "We may well leave the statement in the judicious indefiniteness in which it is expressed by Matthew;" or with Olshausen, who says that the expression that the star stood over the house "was the natural conception of their childish feeling." Every boy knows that a star seems to move when he moves, and to stop when he stops.

The Magi themselves have also been the objects of many wonderful legends. Tradition says there were three of them, and gives their names as Caspar, Melchior, and Balthazar. It was said that their ages were respectively sixty, forty, and twenty, representing three important epochs of human life. It was said again that they came from the then known three great divisions of the globe, Europe, Asia, and Africa, to signify that the whole world had an interest in that infant.

Accordingly in many church pictures one of them is a black man. Raphael followed this tradition in his famous picture of the "Adoration of the Magi," in the Loggia in the Vatican; and his example has been imitated by many artists. Something significant was found in the gifts: the gold being a fit present to a king such as Jesus was to be; the frankincense was suitable for the worship which was everywhere to be offered in his name; and the myrrh foretokened the embalming of his body given for the world's redemption. An old Latin hymn sums this all up as follows: —

"Aurea nascenti fuderunt munera regi,
Thura dedere Deo, myrrhamque tribuere sepulto."

In the old world paintings the Magi are sometimes pictured with crowns on their heads; but more frequently they are represented as wearing oriental turbans. Camels and elephants are occasionally introduced as hints of the far East. Cologne boasts of the honor of possessing their bones; and one of the penances of a visit to that fragrant city is the hearing an old cicerone drawl out the story of the translation of these bones to the banks of the Rhine.

Should it be asked, How was it that those heathen Magi had any correct ideas of the future destiny of this infant? an answer was always near at hand. Of course it was said that they were supernaturally inspired. Even Olshausen says, "These Magi were partly inspired." Kenrick, the American editor of Olshausen, thinks this is hardly enough, and adds in a note, " That the visit of these Magi was accompanied, perhaps, or followed, by the germs of a sincere faith, cannot be doubted." The "perhaps" cannot be doubted.

And then we read, "they fell down and worshipped him." Behold another wonder. These wise men from the East worship Jehovah two weeks old! But even Olshausen was shocked at this, and adds, "We must not by any means ascribe to the Magi any doctrinal ideas of the divinity of Jesus Christ; but only a dim conception of the divine power accompanying and resting on him. We may say they worshipped God who had made this child for salvation to them also; but not the child."

And yet the expression in Matthew is, "they worshipped *him*," the child; and why did not Olshausen say that the original is προσεκύνησαν, which means *show respect*, and has no more to do with worship, in our modern sense of the word, than had their descending from their camels and elephants.

After this glance at the wonderful mysteries and legends connected with St. Matthew's story, the reader will think it a great downfall to the probable facts of the case, in which, as Neander says, "it is not necessary to suppose that any miracle was wrought."

A company of merchants carrying with them the articles in common traffic between the East on the one side, and Judea and Egypt on the other, and travelling, as was common in that hot country, in the cool of the evening, noticed a star which, from the clearness of the air or some aspect of the planets, they had never seen shine so brilliantly. In that age every unusual sight was a sign of something. What did that star mean?

THE SHEPHERDS AND THE MAGI.

Passing near Bethlehem, some rumor, perhaps from the shepherds before named, of the birth of Mary's son, who, as they were told, might be king of the Jews, reached their ears. Here, then, was the meaning of the star. If the Jews were to have a new king they would do homage to him, to propitiate his future protection. That the star was no guide to them is evident from the fact that, on arriving at Jerusalem, they had to ask where the birth of the new king took place, — an inquiry which naturally awakened great surprise at Herod's court.

Starting on their way to Bethlehem, they were rejoiced to see that same planet shining clearly in the heavens, which, as they doubted not, was "his star," the star of the infant king. In their compliments to the mother they named the incident of the star, which little story she remembered, and treasured among her domestic traditions; but it was altogether too unimportant for use with anybody else.

Looking back now upon all these narratives, and tracing them to their probable humble origin, we would ask, Do we destroy their significance? We know that many will think we do, and will add, that we eviscerate the Gospels, strip them of their divine element, and reduce everything to the plane of naturalism.

But we think that the plane of naturalism is God's plane, and it does not seem less divine because it is natural. In these simple events we think we may see the divine hand quite as plainly as in the sun and moon circling round a cradle in Bethlehem. Is it not possible to believe these natural incidents with a depth and sincerity of faith that cannot be accorded to this last named legend, nor to anything like it?

Who is prepared to take the ground that a lowly origin diminishes the importance of a grand result? The heavenly poem of the birth of Jesus, sung all the world over, is it not a heavenly poem still, even if we know out of what simple elements it took its rise? If Dante's "Divina Commedia" originated, as Florentine tradition says, in some spite against that city, is it not the majestic and wonderful poem of the ages for all that? If John Robinson and Elder Brewster got up the expedition to America through some petty misunderstanding with a church in Leyden, is not the settlement of the Plymouth Pilgrims a grand event in history for all that? May not

God's gracious and benignant providence come into connection with human events at any stage of their progress, and in the way He shall judge best? Have we a right to ask that the moment of his contact with them shall be signalized by such prodigies as to our poor eyes may seem most fitting?

There has been by no means a unity of opinion as to the precise time when the divine first mingled with the human element in Jesus. Some have named the moment of his baptism, as did Cerinthus and Basilides, and Theodotus of Byzantium; some, that of his birth; some, that of the salutation of Mary and Elizabeth; some, that of his resurrection; and some, apparently to shut off all curiosity on this point, have held to an "eternal generation," whatever that may mean. Adam Clarke appears to know more about this matter than any one else, for he says, in his "Commentary," that he is "firmly established in the opinion that the rudiments of the human nature of Christ were a real creation in the womb of the virgin," and that Jesus was there filled with the Holy Ghost.

Amid all this diversity of opinion on a subject where it is the height of folly to pretend to know anything, is it not better to abide by the plain words of Scripture, which tell us that Jesus was born like a human being, from a natural father and mother, that he grew up like other children, "increased in wisdom and stature, and in favor with God and man," and received in some period of his life, we know not when or how, but in harmony with the normal action of his own mental and spiritual nature, that spirit which was given to him "without measure," and by which he became fitted for the service he rendered to mankind?

But it may be said that this bald and belittling exegesis does not at all meet the sympathies of the universal human heart, and the most obvious aspects of the case. This may be admitted. But the inquiry is still open whether these "sympathies" be well founded, and whether the "obvious aspect" is not made such by tradition. Our object has not been to find something that will fill the measure of wonder that has been enlarged through long ages of ignorance and credulity, but humbly to suggest a possible explanation of facts which, at the time, were regarded as very simple and not of great importance, but which have since been clothed with the sublimest significance.

Nor let any one regard it as a strange thing that such wonderful interpretations should have been put upon the records of Christ's birth. In past ages men had no other way of marking their sense of something extraordinary in any one, than by the description of extraordinary portents. Thus both Isaac and John the Baptist were said to be miraculously conceived. The Indian Buddha, it was believed, was born of the virgin Maia. Foh, the god of the Chinese, and Shaka, the god of Thibet, were born of virgins. Romulus, it was said, had a human mother, and a god for his father. Plato was begotten by Apollo. Hercules was a son of Jupiter. The mother of Alexander the Great saw in her sleep, just before the birth of her son, a thunderbolt fall upon her body. The mother of Pericles dreamed that she was to give birth to a lion. Here are but a few examples of natal prodigies.

All this is popular language, to express, in the absence of abstract terms and nicely shaded meanings, the idea of something wonderful. Had the career of Washington fallen into the world's history centuries ago, we might have had stories that the chamber of his birth was illuminated with a preternatural light. But we can describe his greatness without the aid of prodigy. Prodigy would not make his patriotism, and wisdom, and disinterestedness seem any greater. We judge him by his life. So the life of Jesus describes him to us, and stamps him as the Son of God and Saviour of the world.

And the simple story of his life may give us a far higher idea of him than is necessarily implied by all the wonders and prodigies attributed to his birth. We see that he who was first regarded merely as the king of Israel has become the Guide and Consoler of humanity; and they who dwelt so much on the fact of the resurrection of his body knew little of the power of that word which would in time roll away the stone from every sepulchre in the world.

"Jésus a été le Messie et a vaincu la mort dans un sens bien plus réel que celui auquel s'étaient attachés les premiers chrétiens. Ceux-ci ne voyaient en lui que le roi d'Israel, et il est devenu le sauveur et le consolateur des' hommes. Ils s'arrêtaient à la résurrection du corps, et ils n'avaient aucune idée de la puissance avec laquelle la parole de leur maître allait briser la pierre au sépulchre pour se répandre sur la face du monde."[1]

[1] Scherer, *Mélanges d'Histoire Religieuse*.

THE SHEPHERDS AND THE MAGI. 71

But God's plan, as unfolded in the sublime march of centuries, is often misunderstood and misrepresented by the philosophy or passions of a particular age; and we must now see what theories the age succeeding that of the apostles invented.

CHAPTER V.

AFTER THEORIES.

IF we have suggested a probable explanation of the account of the birth of Jesus, the question will naturally arise, How came it to be so misrepresented? In what way was a knowledge of his natural birth lost to the world? In what way came the history to be enveloped with the prodigies which are still believed?

At the end of a preceding chapter it was said that we all know how, and when, and where this misinterpretation of the record took place; and it is our purpose now to show this. The subject requires some details of ecclesiastical history. Remembering how tedious these are to most readers, we shall select only a few of the most interesting points, and shall dismiss them with all the brevity compatible with a clear statement of the case.

No one can give even a brief glance into the history of the early ages of the Christian Church without seeing that there were causes then at work to lead to new and high strained theories about the person of Christ, and as a consequence to ascribe peculiar honor to his mother.

1. The first was what was called the offense of the cross. That the founder of their religion had suffered an ignominious death was perpetually thrown into the face of the first Christians. It had been cast as a reproach to St. Paul; but St. Paul did not attempt to evade or mitigate the charge. No high-sounding words, such as soon came into fashion, did he use to cover up the odium of the cross, or to give a factitious splendor to the sacrifice there made. With him it was Jesus of Nazareth, " made of a woman," Galatians iv. 4; "the man Christ Jesus," 1 Timothy ii. 5, who suffered in our behalf; and he gloried in the cross of Christ, and determined to " know nothing but Jesus and him crucified."

Would that his successors had done so! But they set to work to blunt the edge of this charge by their representations of the person of him who was crucified. The greater his dignity, the more the cross was invested with interest. This was their reasoning; but it only showed their inability to penetrate to the true greatness of Christ.

That a superhuman being could meet death with calm self-sacrifice, was not the fact that covered the cross with its transcendent glory. The spiritual significance of the cross lies in the truth that human weakness there found an almighty strength and support. Accordingly St. Paul knew nothing but *Jesus* and him crucified. But some of his successors knew a great deal more than that. It is not long before we find the expressions, God himself suffered, God himself was crucified, God himself died. Texts of Scripture were strangely perverted to give a color to these astounding representations, which found some support in Indian incarnations, and Olympian mythology.

If Jesus were God, how could mortal parents give him birth? The exigency demanded some other explanation. These artless narratives that took their shape from peculiarities of Hebrew phraseology, invited mystic interpretations. These led to the ascription to Mary of a superhuman relation. She became the Queen of Heaven and the object of prayer.

2. The transference of Christianity to lands where the real meaning of its birth-phrases was little understood helped on this tendency. The

overthrow of Jerusalem in the year 70, after one of the most awful sieges recorded in history, drove away the Christian Church from "the mother of us all," and foreign cities became the centres from which the Gospel radiated.

Who of us has adequately considered what must have been the natural effect of taking the religion from its cradle, from the habits of thought and expression where it had its rise, and planting it under new skies, and amid foreign tendencies and customs and speech? It was inevitable that other elements should mingle with it, and that it should receive a deep impress from the place to which it was transferred.

The point is so obvious that it hardly needs illustration; but if we suppose that a new system of philosophy should spring up in Boston, and should be set forth, not in the language of the learned, but in the common phrases, the idioms, the proverbs, the traditional expressions peculiar to New England. who does not see that, if it should be transplanted to another land, and other people, a thousand miles distant, it would naturally be interpreted by the speech, the spirit, the traditions of the new place, and would necessarily be set forth in a light different in many respects from what it had in Boston? We must interpret history by what we know of human nature, and of the inevitable effect of diverse ideas and culture.

It is of much interest in this connection to mark the fact that the farther the Gospel traveled from the influence of its home, the more its records were misunderstood. The great names in Church history which have made Antioch, Cappadocia, Ephesus, Constantinople, so celebrated, were arrayed against the wild speculations to which Alexandria in Egypt gave birth. Mosheim, in his "Historical Commentaries on the State of Christianity during the first Three Hundred and Twenty-five Years of the Christian Era," says, " Nearly all those corruptions by which, in the second and subsequent centuries, Christianity was disfigured, and its pristine simplicity and innocence were almost wholly defaced, had their origin in Egypt, and were thence communicated to other churches." [1]

Let us mark, also, another suggestive fact, namely, that on the subject of the person of Christ the fundamental difference between the northern and southern side of the Mediterranean

[1] Murdock's *Mosheim*, vol. i., p. 369.

was, as is stated in the words of Neander, that the latter believed that "God became a man, while the former believed that God exerted an influence on a man." The profound significance of this discrimination will arrest the attention of the reader.[1]

Neander proceeds still farther to define the theological speculations of the third and fourth centuries, by saying that it was the aim of the Syrian divines to find " in the union of God with man in Christ something analogous to the relation of God to rational beings generally; to find a point of comparison between the being of God in Christ and the being of God in believers;"

[1] See Neander, Boston edition, vol. ii., p. 435. Dupin had before pointed out the same difference between the Syrian and Egyptian churches. He says: "Les Orientaux se sont toujours plus appliqués à marquer la distinction des deux natures en Jésus-Christ que leur intime union, au lieu que les Egyptiens se sont plus attachés à parler de leur union que de leur distinction." French edition, vol. ii., p. 28.

While this book has been under preparation I have used both the original French edition of Dupin, entitled *Nouvelle Bibliothèque des Auteurs Ecclésiastiques*, Mons, 1681, and an English translation published in London, 1692. My quotations in French are from the former; when in English they are from the latter work. I have great respect for the candor of Dupin. He was of the Romish Church, and wrote long prior to the controversies which at the present time bias our minds.

while, on the other hand, as he adds, " the supra-rational and supernatural was precisely that for which the Alexandrian theology chiefly insisted. The ineffable, incomprehensible, transcendent mystery consisted in this very thing, that divine omniscience and human ignorance, human sensibility and suffering and divine exemption from suffering, and in general divine and human attributes, coexisted in one and the same Christ." Vol. ii., p. 445.

If we think that this was equivalent to saying that a square and a circle have the same form, we can hardly be surprised that here in Alexandria should be coined the expression which made such a strife in those ages, that the Virgin Mary was θεοτόκος, that is, the Mother of God.

Mary, the Mother of God? Who can imagine that such an expression should be found in the writings of the apostles? It is evident that they felt no special interest in her; not indeed so much as we might think they should have felt. After Jesus on the cross had commended her to the care of John, and the beloved disciple had taken her, as we are told in John xix. 27, " to his own home," not one word is said of her in the Gospels, nor in the sermons of the first preachers of Christianity, nor in the epistles that were sent to the churches. The one only place where she is even named is in the list of believers in Christ that assembled in the upper room after his crucifixion, and here she is named as " the mother of Jesus," and is included " with the women." Acts i. 14.

We have other most interesting and precious remains of the first followers of Jesus. I refer to the Roman catacombs. Every one knows the story about them. Those dismal subterranean abodes to which the persecuted Christians fled, where they lived till the time of peril had passed, where they buried their dead, and rudely carved many Christian emblems, show us who and what were the historical figures of chief interest to those who had been driven to " dens and caves of the earth."

There they engraved the form of Christ as the Good Shepherd, and the fish, the Greek word of which, ἰχθύς, contained the initials so dear to them (Jesus Christ, Son of God, Saviour), and the anchor, emblem of their hope and trust, and the ship, which represented the Church, to bear them safely over all the storms of life. Thousands of these inscriptions have been carefully removed from the dark and damp catacombs, and are now inserted in the walls of a long corridor in the Vatican, and few objects in Rome are more interesting than the "Lapidary Gallery."

But no image of Mary is there. Pictures of the Virgin and Child are of far later date. The effigies of some Christian matron, found on sarcophagi and in the catacombs, have been claimed by papists as representations of the mother of Jesus; but in the light of the ecclesiastical literature of the first centuries, the claim is preposterous. Not before the fifth century did art multiply images of the Virgin and Child.[1] There is reason to think that such images originated in Egypt, as in some of the oldest statues of the virgin she is represented as being black, in imitation, as is supposed, of the black Egyptian Isis, who, before the times of Christianity, was worshiped as nursing a child. What would those devout souls of the catacombs have thought of the expression, *Mary the Mother of God, the Queen of Heaven, the proper object of prayer?*

[1] Maitland, in his *Church in the Catacombs*, says: "It is a fact notorious to every one conversant with ecclesiastical history, that the Virgin Mary was scarcely noticed in writings, paintings, or sculptures, till late in the fourth century." Page 332.

Let us ask a still more interesting question, What would the first Christians in the mother Church at Jerusalem have thought of this? We are not without means of answering that question. Though the destruction of Jerusalem drove the Christian Church to make settlements in foreign cities, it did not expel from Judea all the followers of Christ. A body of them remained. A little town beyond the Jordan, called Pella, received many of them; and they and their scattered brethren were known under the name of Ebionites, from the fact of their poverty, the Hebrew word אֶבְיוֹן, *Eboon*, meaning poor. What chiefly distinguished them was their belief that the Mosaic system had not been entirely abrogated by Christ, many rites of which they continued to observe. Hence they were sometimes called Judaizers, and were classed as heretics.

It seems not improbable that they might know far better than the Alexandrian mystics what the gospel account of Christ's birth really meant. At any rate, it is certain that they did not believe in his miraculous conception as it was interpreted in Egypt, and continues to be interpreted to this day. They had a Hebrew copy of the Gospel, in which the family memoirs of

Zacharias, and of Joseph and Mary, were left out. The fact which we have here signalized, namely, that they did not believe in the supernatural birth of Jesus, but accounted him as the son of Joseph and Mary, is admitted by all ecclesiastical historians; and the significance of this fact will not escape the notice of any attentive reader.[1]

3. The prevalence of the Manichean philosophy was another cause that aided the dogma of the miraculous birth of Christ. This was a branch of that Gnostic system which ascribed all evil to matter. Spirit and matter were regarded as the two antagonistic principles of the universe. Sin

---

[1] Hagenbach says in his *History of Doctrines*, vol. i., p. 180, that some of the Ebionites believed that a higher power rested on Christ which made him rank with Adam, Enoch, and Moses, and this was the highest conception that they had of him. Mosheim's words are as follows: "Although they [the Ebionites] held our Saviour Jesus Christ in great veneration as a divine legate or prophet, they would not admit that any miraculous circumstances attended his birth, but maintained that he was the natural son of Joseph, begotten according to that law by which all other mortals are produced."

Milman says that the Ebionites not only maintained that Christ was born in the natural way, but affirmed that such was "the unbroken tradition of the Church from the apostles to their own day." See *Latin Christianity*, vol. i., p. 40.

had a self-subsistent existence in matter. As man is allied to matter by his body, he will find his perfection only by mortifying, starving, and scourging it. Here was the origin both of monkish asceticism, and of that dualism, God and Nature, which has been transmitted down to our day. Under this system it became a necessity to show that Christ's sinlessness came from the fact that he had no connection with matter.

Never was the force of theory more signally illustrated. Some, like the Docetæ, taught that Christ had a body only in appearance. Only a phantom had been born and crucified. It had none of the substance of which our bodies are composed. It was incapable alike of sin and of suffering. It was against this opinion that St. John leveled some of his most pointed sentences, condemning those who had denied that Christ had come *in the flesh*, and calling such antichrist. See 1 John iv. 3.

Others maintained that Christ had a real body, but it was not composed of common fleshly matter; it was not derived from Mary; it was fashioned from subtle and celestial materials; it was put together in heaven, according to the belief of Marcion; and it passed through the body of

Mary, as the Bardesanists maintained, as a beam of light passes through glass, or as water passes through a pipe. The fourth and fifth centuries abounded with edifying speculations of this kind, and all these served still more to shape a theology which removed Jesus from any natural alliance with humanity.

4. A fourth cause which contributed to this result was certain metaphysical speculations as to the origin of souls. A subject of which a human being has no knowledge, and can have none except by express revelation, was then treated as if it were all as well understood as the pedigree of one's father, and as if there must be something culpable in dissent.

The historian Gibbon, in a note to his forty-seventh chapter, enumerates the four different opinions that have prevailed: 1. That souls are eternal and divine. 2. That they are created in a separate state of existence before their union with the body. 3. That each soul is created and embodied in the moment of conception. 4. That souls are propagated from the original stock of Adam, who contained in himself the spiritual as well as the corporeal seed of his posterity.

This last opinion took root in the age we are

now considering. Neander gives Tertullian the honor of its paternity, and refers to him as that "great church teacher who in many respects may be regarded as the forerunner of Augustine;" and he adds that it was Tertullian's belief "that our first parent bore within him the undeveloped germ of all mankind; that the soul of the first man was the fountain-head of all human souls, and that all the varieties of individual human nature are but different manifestations of that one spiritual substance. Hence the whole race became corrupted in its original father, and sinfulness is propagated at the same time with souls." [1]

Even if there be the least plausibility in this hypothesis, still it might be asked how was Christ free from all hereditary taint if he derived his being through a human mother? And here came in another assumption. It was maintained that the generative power belongs exclusively to the father, the mother having only a subordinate part in the production of children. See Lecky's "History of Morals," vol. ii., p. 296, who says that we find this notion also among the old Greek writers, for Euripides puts it into the mouth of Apollo in

[1] Neander, vol. 1., p. 615.

the "Eumenides." St. Thomas Aquinas believed it, and hence argued that we ought to love our fathers more than our mothers. But human affections do not always obey this logic.

Reasoning then precisely as some theologians reason still, it was contended that if Jesus had been a son of Joseph he would have inherited the sin of Adam. In all the resources of omnipotence God had no other way of cutting off that sinful connection except by preventing Joseph's coöperation. This was arguing in rather a high strain, and assuming to know much about the resources of omnipotence. But it answered its purpose, and we shall see that some theologians talk in the same style now.

Some of the Schoolmen framed another ingenious theory. They supposed there was a double conception, which we find thus described by Bunsen: "First a conception by which the body was formed, and second that which occurs at the end of forty days when the soul is added to it. The former is called the active, the latter the passive conception. The first took place with Mary in the same manner as with all other human beings; but in the moment of the latter, God delivered the soul that was entering the womb from original sin by a special miracle."[1]

All these baseless hypotheses had one object in view. The aim was to shut out Jesus from any organic connection with humanity; and it was no matter how fanciful and extravagant the opinion might be if only it prepared the way for an admission of a supernatural birth.

5. That birth found a fifth support in the rising clamor in favor of celibacy. All through the Old Testament ages, marriage was in such esteem that one wife did not satisfy the sense of its value. The command at the creation to be fruitful and multiply was well remembered, and the Hebrew spirit uttered itself in the words of Psalm cxxvii. 3, "Lo children are an heritage of the Lord; happy is the man that hath his quiver full of them." Wedlock was a pure and holy state with Jewish priests and the first Christian pastors. In the Epistle to the Hebrews xiii. 4, marriage is called "honorable in all;" and in the First Epistle to Timothy iv. 3, among the doctrines of devils which would come in, in the latter times, St. Paul names this, "forbidding to marry."

[1] Bunsen's *God in History*, vol. iii., p. 158.

As late as the beginning of the fourth century St. Jerome called the whole book of Solomon's Song an indubitable proof in favor of marriage, and he names bishops who would ordain none but married men. St. Augustine wrote a treatise "De Bono Conjugale," denying that celibacy had any special merit of itself, though praising it when chosen in a right spirit; and Jovinian of Verona, whom Neander calls the Protestant of the fifth century, set himself against the frenzy of his times, and defended the honorableness and desirableness of marriage.

If any one is curious to know how an opinion in favor of celibacy sprung up, and what connection it had with various heathen superstitions, with Manichean speculations, and metaphysical notions about the origin of souls, he may find much light in the "Historical Sketch of Sacerdotal Celibacy," by Henry C. Lea, Philadelphia, 1867, a learned and thorough work, to which we have been indebted.

Celibacy was at first severely denounced by the Church. The Apostolical Constitutions probably reflected the spirit of their times, and with an unexpected degree of good sense, they said, "Nam nec legitimus concubitus, nec cubile, nec sanguinis fluxus, nec nocturna pollutio, potest hominis naturam contaminare, vel spiritum sanctum auferre ; sed sola impietas et actio injusta." And again, " Nuptæ igitur honestæ et commendabiles sunt, ipsaque liberorum procreatio pura est, nihil enim mali est in bono."

Pope Syricus, A. D. 385, was the first to enjoin celibacy, asking, " Can the Spirit dwell in any other than holy bodies ? " as though, says Neander, " true holiness is incompatible with marriage." Twenty years after this, Pope Innocent I. decreed that all married priests should be deprived of office. Success could attend such steps only by the most extravagant laudations of the virtue of the single state, and Cyprian got up a mathematical comparison of it to martyrdom, which he rated at one hundred and celibacy at sixty ; and Chrysostom pronounced virginity as much superior to marriage as heaven is to earth, or as angels are to men.

To support the opinion in favor of perpetual virginity resort was also had to wonders revealed from the spiritual world ; and it is in this age that occurred, it is said, the incident of St. Julian and St. Basilissa, which we find reported as follows in one of the old legends of the Church :

Forced by his parents to take a spouse, Julian was inspired by God to select Basilissa, who was of the same mind as himself, namely, that after marriage they would live only as the angels in heaven. On the nuptial night Jesus Christ appeared to the holy couple, and he and his august mother, escorted by a legion of virgins, filled the chamber with the celestial light of their presence, and with the odor of lilies and roses, though it was midwinter, and brought two golden crowns, and said, "Victory to you, Julian; victory to you, Basilissa! Exalted shall be your place in heaven, grand shall be your glory, brilliant shall be your crowns!" And the Church recognized and proclaimed the triumph by giving the title of saints to these two virgin souls.

But even with all these, mathematics, rhetoric, and fable, the papal decrees were a failure. The well-known lines of Horace, about trying to expel nature, must have often come to mind.[1] For six or eight centuries the subject was a fruitful source of trouble. If the reader should ever turn over the pages of Dupin's "Ecclesiastical

---

[1] "Naturam expellas furcâ, tamen usque recurret,
    Et mala perrumpet furtim fastidia victrix."
A terrible meaning must have been often found in these lines.

History," where are summaries of the decisions of all the leading Church Councils, he will get a vivid idea of the vast amount of discussion that must have been given to this subject.

" This overstrained demand on the virtue, not of individuals in a high state of enthusiasm, but of a whole class of men ; this strife with nature in that which, in its irregular and lawless indulgence, is the source of so many evils and so much misery, in its more moderate and legal form is the parent of the purest affections and the holiest charities; this isolation from those social ties, which, if at times they might draw them from total dedication to their sacred duties, in general would, by their tending to soften and humanize, be the best school for the gentle and affectionate discharge of those duties ; this enforcement of the celibacy of the clergy was not slow in producing its inevitable evils. Simultaneously with the sterner condemnation of marriage, or at least the exaggerated praises of chastity, we hear the solemn denunciations of the law against those secret evasions by which the clergy endeavored to obtain the fame without the practice of celibacy, — to enjoy some of the pleasures without the crime of marriage. From the middle of the third century, in which the growing aversion to the marriage of the clergy begins to appear, we find the "sub-introduced" females constantly proscribed. The intimate union of the priest with a young, often a beautiful, female, who still passed to the world under the name of a virgin, and was called by the priest by the unsuspected name of a sister, seems, from the strong and reiterated language of Jerome, Gregory Nazianzen, Chrysostom, and others, to have been almost general." [1]

Not often was the controversy redeemed by such gleams of good sense as St. Ulric showed, who, in 952, when a council was held at Augsburg which tried to enforce celibacy, addressed a long letter to the pope, Agapetus II., in which he said: "How much more obnoxious to divine wrath are the promiscuous and nameless crimes indulged in by those who would enforce celibacy, than the chaste and single marriages of the clergy;" and then when, alluding to the "violent distortion of the sacred texts by those who sought authority to justify the laws," he not unhappily characterized it as "straining the breast

[1] Milman's *History of Christianity*, book iv., chapter 1.

of Scripture until it yielded blood instead of milk."[1]

Let us pass over the petitions sent by laymen begging that the clergy might be allowed to marry, as this might protect the purity of households committed to their spiritual charge; as also the secular consideration that favored celibacy, namely, the vast sums of money bequeathed to the Church for religious uses, but squandered by the clergy on their children. The Church, it was believed, would be richer if the clergy "were relieved of the cares of paternity," to adopt the euphemism of those times.

It is a sad history, and a disgraceful history, and the struggle is a sad and disgraceful one in the Romish Church to this day. How fruitful of warning to those who would set themselves in array against the laws of our nature! The connection of this subject with the point under discussion lies in the fact, that in all this long and scandalous controversy, the virginity of the mother of Christ, and the supposed continence of Joseph, were matters of unceasing laudation; and all this helped to fasten upon the accounts of

[1] Lea's *Sacerdotal Celibacy*, p. 153.

the birth of Jesus the interpretations which have been handed down to this day.

And now comes the fight. For fight there was between the more moderate and more scriptural interpretations of the north of the Mediterranean, and the fiery and impetuous fanaticism of Alexandria. In no other struggle in all Christian history have theological odium, and sectarian hot-headedness, and partisan diplomacy, and blood-thirsty measures made a more striking display. Some of the chief points in this picturesque but shameful controversy we shall present in the next chapter. As we have now seen by what means the primitive records of Christ's birth came to be overlaid by false interpretations, so we shall next mark how these interpretations were forced into the line of Christian tradition, and were established as the orthodoxy of the Church.

CHAPTER VI.

THE FIGHT.

THE difference in opinion, on the subject of the nature of Christ, between the northern and southern side of the Mediterranean, has been summed up generally by Neander, in words which we have quoted in a former chapter, as follows: The Syrian churches held that God exerted an influence on a man; the Egyptian churches held that God became a man.

Of course it will be understood that the Syrian theologians explained themselves in divers manners, and had themselves more or less departed from the simplicity of the sacred writers, who contented themselves with calling Jesus the Son of God, the promised Messiah, the Sent of the Father, the Saviour of the world; while, in the fifth century, there was everywhere a disposition to go beyond these words, — a prurient desire to pry into the nature of Christ, and to apply to him high-sounding titles. This tendency had been apparent for a hundred years, and had been signally displayed in the Council at Nice in 325, when there had been a fierce and successful struggle to supplant the simplicity of the evangelical statements by mysterious metaphysical subtleties.

But the excess to which the Egyptian theologians carried this tendency was at length intolerably revolting to the more sober thought of the Syrian Christians; and when, in Alexandria, was applied to the Virgin Mary the expression θεοτόκος, Mother of God, it was like casting a firebrand into an inflammable mass. Let us mark some of the circumstances which conspired to kindle the flames that soon raged.

Alexandria was then one of the most prominent cities of the world. Founded by Alexander the Great 332 B. C., its advantageous position at the mouth of the Nile gave it a rapid growth, an early commercial importance, and a population at one time surpassing that of Rome. History tells us of its immense trade between Europe and the far East, — a trade afterwards diverted by the discovery of the passage round the Cape of Good Hope, but in our times regained, at least in part, by the construction of the Suez Canal.

But we are more interested in its then multiform intellectual culture. It became the home of scholars and disputants from all parts of the world, and Egyptian mysteries, and Greek sophism, and Jewish theocracy, and Persian philosophy, and Indian subtleties, strove for the mastery in the fervid life favored by the mercurial spirit of the people and the place. Here the Old Testament had been translated from the Hebrew into Greek, in the version known as the Septuagint; here were the great libraries so famous in history; and here flourished the men whose names make such a figure in ecclesiastical writings, — Philo, Porphyry, Clement, Origen, Athanasius, Cyril.

What would become of the religion of Jesus when thrown into that seething Alexandrian cauldron? Christianity must have something more mysterious, incomprehensible, than any other system if it would there gain favor. The obscure origin of its founder was an offense in the eyes of ambitious sectarists. But those records of his birth had great capabilities. Something might be made out of them more wonderful than Grecian mythology or Indian incarnations could parallel.

It seems probable that a peculiar notion of the Egyptian philosophers here rendered some aid. Plutarch tells us, in his life of Numa, that "the wise Egyptians held that it may be possible for a divine spirit so to apply itself to the nature of a woman as to imbreed in her the first beginnings of generation," without any intercourse with man. Here may have been the genetic idea of the whole Alexandrian scheme, and of the theology thence derived.

The tone of mind then prevailing at Alexandria was one which has shown itself in many ages, and may be recognized at this present time among the Ritualists in England, and those in other places who sympathize with them. The more wonderful and incomprehensible the dogmas and rites of religion are made, the more it suits the taste to which we refer. And this taste must continually have something new to feed it, and hence there is a rapid progress in extravagance. To those who renounce the guide of the judgment, and appeal wholly to a love of the marvelous, learning is nothing but a hindrance, common sense a carnal intruder, and the man of empty brain, with lighted candles and sing-song tone, is as good as anybody, on a level with well-furnished and enlightened minds, — perhaps a little better, for there is no suspicion that he has wit enough to see the hollow delusion.

In his Lectures on "Ecclesiastical History," Dr. Campbell says : "To men of shallow understanding, theological paradoxes afford a pleasure not unlike, that which is derived from being present at the wonderful feats of jugglers. In these, by mere sleight of hand, one appears to do what is impossible to be done; and in those, by mere sleight of tongue (in which the judgment has no part), an appearance of meaning and consistency is given to terms the most self-contradictory, and the incredible seems to be rendered worthy of belief. To set fools a-staring is alike the aim of both. Of the two kinds of artifice, the juggler's and the sophist's, the former is much the more harmless."

The patriarch of Alexandria, at the time to which we now come, was Cyril, a man of unfailing cunning and tact, united to boundless ambition, and prompt and arrogant force. He had been elevated to the episcopal throne in 412, and had exercised with a high hand the large temporal powers which his position gave him. His character will come out with sufficient distinctness. At the head of a fanatical rabble he assailed the quarter of the city assigned to the Jews, then numbering forty thousand souls, who had there long lived in peace. Their synagogues he tore down, and their goods he gave to the plunder of his soldiers.[1]

His connection with the thrilling fate of the beautiful and accomplished Hypatia has often been described. She had applied herself to the study of philosophy, had acquired distinction in Athens as a scholar, and when still a young woman, had been invited to take charge of one of the principal schools in Alexandria, where her lectures drew crowds of admirers. Her great personal attractions, her learning, the unblemished purity of her life, made her extremely popular in the city; but her refusal to declare herself a Christian — a refusal which did her honor, considering what the word "Christian" then meant — marked her out as a victim of religious fanaticism.

[1] Josephus says that Alexandria, in his time, was half a Jewish city. The part of the city which the Jews inhabited was called the *Delta*. Here they formed a sort of republic, administering their own affairs, rendering justice, attending to the execution of contracts and testaments, as in an independent state. — Josephus, *Antiq.*, xviii. 9.

Of course, it is impossible at this day to apportion aright the guilt of her murder. Gibbon charges it upon Cyril, as did Theodoret, a church historian of the fifth century, and an anti-Nestorian. Gibbon says: "On a fatal day, in the holy season of Lent, Hypatia was torn from her chariot, stripped naked, dragged to the church, and inhumanly butchered by the hands of Peter the reader, and a troop of savage and merciless fanatics; her flesh was scraped from her bones with sharp oyster shells, and her quivering limbs were given to the flames. The just progress of inquiry and punishment was stopped by seasonable gifts; but the murder of Hypatia has imprinted an indelible stain on the character and religion of Cyril of Alexandria."[1] Chapter xlvii.

[1] An interesting sketch of her life may be found in Chateaubriand's *Études Historiques*, who also imputes the guilt of her murder to Cyril. Hypatia is the heroine of one of Charles Kingsley's historical romances. The bold and blunt Jortin sums up the case of Cyril and Hypatia in these words: "Cyril was strongly suspected of having been an instigator of her murder. Dupin and Lowth endeavor to vindicate him; but though there is not sufficient evidence to condemn him, yet neither is there room to acquit him. Neither Socrates nor Valesius have dropped one word in his vindication. Philostorgius says that Hypatia was murdered by the Consubstantialists, and Damasius

Triumphs at home awakened his ambition for conquests abroad. The other side of the Mediterranean offered a wider field. He had had aspirations to the patriarchate of Constantinople. Foiled there, he did not mean to sink into a subordinate position. Was not Alexandria too large a place to play a secondary part?[1]

says it was done at the instigation of Cyril." — Jortin's *Remarks on Ecclesiastical History.*

One crime more or less weighs little in the condemnation of a man like Cyril. In regard to his conduct in the murder of Hypatia, Jortin goes too far when he says that Dupin endeavors to vindicate him. Dupin calls Hypatia an illustrious woman, whose reputation for learning extended so far that students flocked to her lectures from all parts, and says that her friendship for Orestes, the Governor of Alexandria, an open enemy of Cyril, made her hateful to this bishop. Dupin, indeed, says: " Saint Cyrille n'eut aucune part à ce meurtre," referring to the act itself, but not screening him from guilt in its preparation, for Dupin adds that the assassination was by this prelate's friends; and they probably well knew what would be agreeable to him. — *Dupin,* vol. iv., p. 41.

[1] " Some jealousy which at that time subsisted respecting the relative dignity of the two sees of Alexandria and Constantinople probably heightened the contention, and is believed by some to have caused it." These are feeble words found in Waddington's *Church History.* The truth is, this jealousy had been long implacable, and Cyril was confident that the Roman pontiff favored the claims of Alexandria. Out of hatred to Constantinople, the successive popes accorded superiority to the Egyp-

Was his church, founded by St. Mark, to yield to that of Constantinople which had grown up wholly by secular causes? Was not the difference in their theology an opportunity to "mount the whirlwind and direct the storm?"

In reading history of any kind, ecclesiastical or civil, we must not make the mistake of supposing that the causes assigned for controversies and wars *create* the passions which are soon displayed. The passions existed before the struggle, and seek the object by which they may express themselves. The two Italian towns which carried on a murderous war against each other, alleged as a reason that the artists of one represented the eyes of the dead Christ as open, against the orthodox fashion of the other who painted them as shut; but every one knew that

---

tian see. The quarrel between Alexandria and Constantinople was further embittered by the aims of both to have supremacy over all the churches of the East. "L'Evêque de Constantinople vouloit être le maître des Diocèses d'Asie et de Pont; celui d'Alexandrie les lui disputoit, et vouloit même soûmettre à sa jurisdiction une partie de l'Orient." Dupin, vol. iv., p. 327.

What scenes of intrigue, bribery, violence, and bloodshed had long marked the relations between Constantinople and Alexandria, may be seen in an able book, *St. Jean Chrysostome*, par Amédé Thierry, Paris, 1872.

here was only the pretext, and that back of this they had many old scores to settle.

The pretext for wars grows out of subjects which interest the world at the time. In epochs of national aggrandizement it is some question of a boundary; in ages of martial glory it is some point of military ambition; in commercial eras it is some infraction of the interests of trade. In the fifth century, when religious discussions were the world's great employment, it was a question whether Mary was the Mother of God. But in all these cases the passion is back of the object, and the alleged cause is only a pretext.[1]

---

[1] The long Arian controversy which raged so fiercely for centuries, presents a memorable example of the difference between pretext and cause. Men said that they fought for the truth; but it is incredible that ignorant hordes of barbarians understood the merits of the discussion about δmooousian and δmoiousian. It is not always understood even by learned men now. The intense hatred of Arianism must have been fed by political and national rancor. Dean Stanley, in his *Lectures on the Eastern Churches*, p. 173, says that the chief cause of the opposition to Arianism was its "making two Gods instead of one, and thus relapsing into Polytheism." No opinion can appear stranger than this. Early and late in the controversy the Trinitarians were charged with making three Gods instead of one, and thus relapsing into Polytheism. In twenty-two years after the Council of Nice, a large Council at Sardis anathematized the tritheistic tendencies of believers in the Nicene Creed. So,

Constantinople was the head-quarters of the party opposed to Cyril. Fanaticism was the disease of the age, and Constantinople had its share. Gregory of Nyssa gives a vivid picture of the rage in that city for doctrinal disputes. "Every nook and corner of the city," he says, "is full of men who discuss incomprehensible subjects. They are found in the streets, the markets, among the people who sell old clothes, those who sit at the tables of the money-changers, and those who deal in provisions. Ask a man how many oboli a thing comes to, he gives you a specimen of dogmatizing on generated and ungenerated being. Inquire the price of bread, you are answered, the Father is greater than the Son, and the Son subordinate to the Father. Ask if the bath be ready, you are answered, the Son of God was created from nothing."[1]

The patriarch of Constantinople at that time

in modern times, Arianism has never been thought to impair the unity of God. On the other hand, Trinitarianism has always been prone to relapse into Polytheism. As to the real cause of the internecine strife between these two early forms of Christianity, much, no doubt, was due to the struggle for the approval of the civil power, as non-acceptance of its religious belief was treason, and was punishable as such.

[1] Quoted by Neander, vol. ii., p. 388.

was Nestorius. He had been brought up in the cloisters of Antioch, and had been raised, by his austere life and impetuous eloquence, to be head of the church at " a corrupt court where every species of intrigue and passion was busily at work." Neander, from whom we quote this, alludes to him as " destitute of prudence and moderation ; " but this seems a feeble way of characterizing one whose whole career reveals that want of practical tact and ability often seen in men who know nothing except from books.

His obvious weakness invited insults. Once as he was preaching against the doctrine of the generation of the eternal Logos, and contrasting it with the nativity of Christ as the divine instrument, he was interrupted by some crack-brained fanatic who exclaimed, " No, the Eternal Logos himself condescended to the second birth ; " and the church became the scene of one of those commotions of clapping and stamping for which Constantinople was then celebrated. At another time, as he was entering the church to preach in his usual style, a monk confronted him, declaring that " a heretic ought not to be allowed to teach in public."

In Alexandria the cry was, " Let him be ac-

THE FIGHT. 107

cursed who says 'Mary is not the Mother of God.'" In Constantinople the cry was, "How can God be born? Who could say of the infant Jesus, God was two hours or two days old? Accursed be he who vents such blasphemy! Mary was χριστότοκος, that is, Mother of Christ."[1] And then we have a long account in Church History of the cunning measures of Cyril to fan the rising flame, of the spies and bribes[2] that he

[1] Early in the last century some papists, who thought it was time to start some new wonderful phraseology, began to call the mother of the Virgin Mary, Anna, "The Grandmother of God." The Pope, Clement XI., forbade this, as he believed it would be offensive to the Christian world. Dr. Campbell, in his *Lectures on Ecclesiastical History*, in recording these facts, adds, "It is impossible for one, without naming Nestorius, to give a clearer decision in his favor." But to have called Anna the grandmother of God would have awakened no sense of impropriety in the fifth century. The second Council of Nice called the Apostle James "God's brother." The phrase, "Mother of God," touched some chivalrous sensibilities of the age when it was first used, and it is impossible to explain its effect until we take this into account. "It was intimately connected," says Dr. Schaff, in his Church History, "with the growing veneration of the Virgin. It therefore struck into the field of devotion which lies much nearer the people than that of speculative theology, and thus it touched the most vehement passions."

[2] Gibbon gives an account of a letter that has been singularly preserved and transmitted down to our times, written by Cyril's archdeacon, containing a list of prominent persons in Constan-

sent to Constantinople, of the popular preachers whom he won over to his side, of the letters and books he wrote, dedicating some to the Emperor Theodosius II., and converting to his views one of the Emperor's sisters, Augusta Pulcheria, a woman of great influence, who had been hurt by some slight of Nestorius.

This hurt might easily happen, for the patriarch was impulsive and rough. By many of the clergy he was hated as a stranger put over them, and most of them joined the party who ascribed the greatest honor to the Virgin.

The little story about Dalmatius is a curious picture of the times. Dalmatius was a monk who for forty-eight years had never left his cell. His reputation for sanctity was so great that the people resorted to his intercessions in every perplexity. Even the Emperor himself had repeatedly visited him to implore his aid. He was an almost omnipotent oracle in that generation. By Alexandrian influence he was won over to Cyril's side, who communicated with him by means of

tinople to whom magnificent bribes had been sent. These bribes must have been numerous as well as costly, for it appears that the clergy of Alexandria mourned over the poverty which the gifts entailed. See Gibbon, 47th chapter, and also Neander, vol. ii., p. 482.

a letter concealed in a hollow reed borne as a staff by a pilgrim.

Dalmatius denounced Nestorius as "an evil beast who had entered the city." He declared that an exigency had now arrived that summoned him to leave his cell. He put himself at the head of a procession of monks and abbots who marched through the streets bearing burning torches and chanting psalms. He demanded that the Emperor should give more heed to "six thousand bishops than to one godless man." He excited the whole city to a state of frenzied madness.

All this encouraged Cyril to a more decisive step. Quarreling bishops in the East had often called for the help of the Pope at Rome, who was anxious then to extend and assure his power. Cyril represented to Celestine I., the reigning pontiff, that now was the favorable moment for him to intervene, and put himself at the head of the party contending for the highest views of the person of Christ. To this end he suggested that a general council should be summoned to settle the points in dispute.

Readers of Church History know what councils have been. One has been held in our day and is of fresh memory. Under the pretense of an inspiration of the Holy Spirit, there have probably been no assemblies of men where worldly ambition, and personal intrigue, and party strife, and national hate, and adulation and bribery, have played a more effective part.

"Nowhere is Christianity less attractive, and, if we look to the ordinary tone and character of the proceedings, less authoritative, than in the Councils of the Church. They are in general a fierce collision of two rival factions, neither of which will yield, each of which is solemnly pledged against conviction. Intrigue, injustice, violence, decisions on authority alone, and that the authority of a turbulent majority, decisions by wild acclamation rather than after sober inquiry, detract from the reverence, and impugn the judgment at least of the later Councils. The close is almost invariably a terrible anathema, in which it is impossible not to discern the tones of hatred, of arrogant triumph, of rejoicing at the damnation imprecated against the humiliated adversary." [1]

The Council summoned to meet in Ephesus "about Pentecost," in the year 431, was nothing but a tool in the hands of Cyril and the fifty

[1] Milman's *Latin Christianity.*

Egyptian bishops, and their numerous attendants, whom in an imposing fleet he had brought with him. It was opened before the prelates of Asia Minor, known to be adverse to the Alexandrian Creed, had arrived. In consequence of inundations impairing the public ways, their progress was delayed. In their absence, Nestorius and sixty-eight bishops refused to be present. The session was held in the great Church of St. Mary. It was Mary's title to the highest honor which they were now determined to maintain. Cyril was president and directed all the proceedings. "It had been skillfully arranged that Ephesus should be chosen for the decision of a difference respecting the dignity of the Virgin, since popular tradition had buried her in that city, and the imperfect Christianity of its inhabitants had readily transferred to her the worship which their ancestors had offered to Diana."[1] There was no pretense at deliberation and argument, for a snap-judgment was pronounced, after a session of only one day.

Their decision, which received one hundred and sixty signatures, is worth quoting. "Our Lord Jesus Christ, by Nestorius blasphemed, has ordained by this most holy synod that the Nesto-

[1] Waddington's *Ch. Hist.*

rius above named should be excluded from the Episcopal dignity, and from the whole college of priests :" and this sentence, which names no charge and adduces no proof, was reached, as was said, with an hypocrisy not altogether unknown in such cases, "after many tears."

This decree was sent " To Nestorius, a second Judas ; " and Cyril immediately had it posted up in Ephesus, proclaimed by heralds, and reëchoed by a crowd of bullies and slaves, whom he had brought into the city to sustain his side by clamors and blows. Illuminations and songs and tumults attested his triumph, and the joy of the city, which claimed the honor of possessing the body of the Virgin.[1]

[1] Of this Council Dupin writes as follows : " There are several objections made against the nature of this Council and the management of it. Some say that it ought to be accounted no better than a tumultuous and rash assembly, where all things were carried by passion and noise, and not an Ecumenical Council ; that St. Cyril held it against the consent of the commissioners whom the emperor sent to call them together ; that not only Nestorius and his party, but also several other orthodox bishops opposed it ; that Cyril scorned to wait for the Eastern bishops, who would soon have arrived, and who desired him to wait for them ; that he did not stay for the legates of the holy see, nor any of the western bishops ; that his synod was made up of the Egyptian bishops and some bishops of Asia who were wholly devoted to his will ; that it was he that did all and

The spirit which animated Cyril's party may be inferred from some of their sayings which have ordered all in the Council. The manner in which he acted against Nestorius, and the rashness he was guilty of in condemning him, make it credible that he was actuated by nothing but passion; that St. Isidore reproved St. Cyril, telling him ' that several persons laughed at him, and at the tragedy which he had acted at Ephesus; that it was said openly that he sought nothing but revenge upon his enemy; that he had better have been quiet and not revenged his private quarrels at the expense of the Church, and raise an eternal discord among Christians under a pretense of piety.' This Council was so far from bringing peace that it brought nothing but trouble, divisions, and scandals into the Church of Jesus Christ, so that that may be said of this Council with a great deal more truth, which St. Gregory Nazianzen said of the Councils of his time, 'that he never saw an assembly of bishops that had a good and happy conclusion; that they always increased the distemper rather than cured it; that the obstinate contests and ambition of domineering which ordinarily reigns among them renders them prejudicial, and generally they who are concerned to judge others, are moved thereto by ill-will, rather than by a desire to restrain faults.' This seems to agree to the Council of Ephesus better than to any other assembly of bishops." Dupin, vol. iv., p. 213. Dupin proceeds to mitigate the force of some of these objections, and finds the central cause of the quarrel in the self-contradictory terms dear to the Egyptian, but offensive to the Oriental bishops. Referring to what St. Gregory Nazianzen here said of Councils, Dr. Campbell adds: "How a man, who, in the fifth century could talk so reasonably and so much like a Christian, came to be sainted, is not indeed to be easily accounted for."

come down to us. One bishop declared that "as those who counterfeit the imperial coin deserve the extremest punishment, so Nestorius, who has presumed to falsify the doctrines of orthodoxy, deserves every punishment both from God and man." Another bishop preached a sermon in which he said, as quoted by Neander, that "Nestorius was worse than Cain and the Sodomites. The earth ought to open and swallow him up; fire ought to rain down on him from heaven. The God Logos whom he had ventured to sever, who had come forth in the flesh from Mary, the Mother of God, would appoint for him the punishment of eternal torments in the day of judgment."

And what was the offense of this man? He believed in the Lord Jesus Christ, as a Teacher sent from God, and the Saviour of the world. But he could not accept the interpretations which Alexandrian fanaticism had put upon the records of Christ's birth. He called Mary the Mother of Christ, and not the Mother of God. For this offense, and as the representative of the prevailing belief of the Syrian churches, he must be crushed.[1]

[1] "Had Nestorius been a better politician, and a more equal

THE FIGHT. 115

When at length the tardy bishops arrived at Ephesus, they were amazed at the precipitancy of Cyril, and proceeded to organize a new Council. They declared that the decision which had been proclaimed was of *ex parte* origin, without validity, and that they themselves, to the number of forty-two bishops, constituted the only regular Council.

But Cyril had got the start of them. He soon brought both the Emperor — a feeble boy, under the influence of his mother and sister — and the Pope to sustain his side. Nestorius was degraded, his books were burned, all meetings of his friends forbidden, and he was driven into exile on one of the oases of Egypt, near the confines of Nubia. Here hordes of Nubian barbarians soon fell upon the place, laying it waste by fire and the

match for his adversary, St. Cyril, the decision of the Church had infallibly been the reverse of what it was; and we should at this day find Cyrilianism in the list of heresies, and a Saint Nestorius in the calendar of the beatified." Campbell's *Lectures on Ecclesiastical History*. "From his sad fate and upright character, Nestorius, after having been long abhorred, has in modern times, since Luther, found much sympathy; while Cyril, by his violent conduct, has incurred much censure. Gieseler and Neander take the part of Nestorius; and Milman said he would rather meet the judgment of the Divine Redeemer loaded with the errors of Nestorius than with the barbarities of Cyril." Schaff.

sword. Nestorius was carried off as a prisoner. By a tool of Cyril the old man was dragged about from place to place under a guard of soldiers. It is not certainly known how death came to his relief. As to Cyril, we may say in the words of Gibbon, that "the title Saint prefixed to his name is a mark that his opinions and his party finally prevailed." [1]

[1] When those who shared the opinions of Nestorius were driven away from Constantinople, some of them fled to the East, and their descendants, taking his name, and establishing churches amid the mountain-fastnesses of Western Persia, exist to this day. They form a distinct line of transmission of the Christian faith, independent of the Romish and Greek churches, and in some respects purer than either. Gibbon is mistaken who speaks of them as "obliterated." The Nestorians number many thousand souls. Though an ignorant and decaying people, they still protest against calling Mary the Mother of God, or addressing her in prayer, or adoring her image. A Nestorian Bishop, Mar Yohannan, came to the United States in 1842. Alexander von Humboldt, in the second volume of his *Cosmos*, says, "It was one of the wondrous arrangements in the system of things that the Christian sect of the Nestorians, which has exerted a very important influence on the geographical extension of knowledge, was of service even to the Arabians before the latter found their way to learned and disputatious Alexandria. The Arabians gained their first acquaintance with Grecian literature through the Syrians, while the Syrians themselves had first received a knowledge of Grecian literature through the anathematized Nestorians."

A triumph where there was no inward conviction, but only an artificial union through fraud and violence — how long would it last? Dupin says: "La paix apparente qui le suivit n'était qu'une paix plâtrée." There were other troubles at hand, and we must glance at them in order to complete our view of the manner in which the Alexandrian theology got its foothold in the Church.[1]

There was in Constantinople an abbot by the name of Eutyches, a warm advocate of the Egyptian dogma, who devised some forms of expression that opened the controversy anew. Taking the words in the Proem of St. John's Gospel in their literal sense, "The Word was God, and the Word was made flesh," he contended not only that Christ was God, but there was nothing in him but God. He had but one nature and that was

[1] In looking back upon this shameful conflict, Milman, in his *History of Christianity*, has some reflections worth reading, though in part quoted on a preceding page. He says: "While ambition, intrigue, arrogance, rapacity, and violence are proscribed as unchristian means; barbarity, persecution, bloodshed, as unholy and unevangelical wickednesses; posterity will condemn the orthodox Cyril as one of the worst of heretics against the spirit of the Gospel. Who would not meet the judgment of the Divine Redeemer loaded with the errors of Nestorius, rather than with the barbarities of Cyril?"

God. Those who said that God dwelt in Christ, divided Christ into two parts, the divine and the human Christ; and this leaves the door open to the suspicion that the last was born in the natural way. This is awful heresy. Accordingly the cry was, " Let those who divide Christ be themselves divided by the sword. Let them be hewn in pieces. Let them be burned alive." [1]

Flavian, the successor of Nestorius, and like him a representative of the Syrian theology, opposed these statements. An appeal was again made to the Pope. The pontiff, Leo the Great, called another Council which met at Ephesus in 449. It is known in history as the "Robber Synod," from its scenes of violence and bloodshed. "A troop of hospital waiters and soldiers," says Neander, "was admitted into the assembly for the purpose of intimidating refractory members. . . . . Force was resorted to in various ways to compel men to assent to the decisions of the Council. Bishops were kept confined in the Church. They were menaced by soldiers and monks till they had subscribed, and blank papers were laid before them for their signature which could afterwards be filled up with whatever the

[1] See Neander, vol. ii., p. 501.

leaders chose." It was thus that the Alexandrian, Eutychian, Monophysite (one nature) doctrine overwhelmed all opposition.[1]

Gibbon gives a picturesque view of this Council. "A furious multitude of monks and soldiers, with staves and swords and chains, burst into the church; the trembling bishops hid themselves behind the altar or under the benches, and as they were not inspired with the zeal of martyrdom, they successively subscribed a blank paper which was afterwards filled with the condemnation of the Byzantine prelate. Flavian was instantly delivered to the wild beasts of this spiritual amphitheatre. It is said that the patriarch

---

[1] It is edifying to see what sensible words a contemporary uttered in regard to the fact that the violent party had the majority on its side. Eutherus was at this time Bishop of Tyana, and with other Syrian prelates manfully combated the Alexandrian theology. When told that the multitude was against him, he asked, in words translated into French: "Mais quelle est cette multitude que vous m'opposez? C'est une troupe de gens corrumpus par les flatteries et par les prisons. C'est un nombre d'ignorans qui n'ont point de lumière pour se conduire. Ce sont une quantité de personnes foibles et timides qui se sont laissées vaincre. Ainsi quand vous m'opposez cette multitude pour autoriser le mensonge, vous ne faites autre chose que de découvrir la grandeur du mal et le grand nombre des misérables." Dupin, vol. iv., p. 68.

of Alexandria reviled and buffeted and kicked and trampled his brother of Constantinople; it is certain that the victim, before he could reach the place of his exile, expired on the third day of the wounds and bruises he had received at Ephesus." Chapter 47.

Two years later still another Council was called to meet at Chalcedon, whose main object it seemed to be to hit upon expressions that would harmonize all parties. As their result has continued to the present time to be the orthodox expression of the nature and person of Christ, it deserves to be here quoted. We find it thus stated by Dupin: " That they did believe in one Lord Jesus Christ, the Son of God, perfect God and perfect man, consubstantial with God as to his divinity, and with man according to his humanity; in whom there are two natures united without change, division, or separation; so that the properties of the two natures do subsist in and agree to one and the same person, who is not divided into two, but is one Jesus Christ."

And thus, as Gibbon says, "the road to Paradise, a bridge as sharp as a razor, was suspended over the abyss by the master-hand of the theological artist. During ten centuries of blindness and servitude, Europe received her religious opinions from the oracle of the Vatican, and the same doctrine, already varnished with the rust of antiquity, was admitted without dispute into the creed of the Reformers, who disclaimed the supremacy of the Roman Pontiff. The Synod of Chalcedon still triumphs in the Protestant churches; but the ferment of controversy has subsided, and the most pious Christians of the present day are ignorant or careless of their belief concerning the mysteries of the incarnation." Chapter 47.

No, not so much "careless of their belief," as blindly following their leaders like sheep. For this decision of the Council of Chalcedon is regarded in some quarters, even at the present day, as the last word which the science of theology can utter. Dr. Shedd, in his "History of Doctrines," says, "Beyond this, the human mind, it is probable, is unable to go in the endeavor to unfold the mystery of Christ's complex person."

If a writer on geology, reverting to the earliest speculations on that science, should claim them as something beyond which the human mind cannot go, what should we think of such a statement as that.[1]

[1] After all, it is worthy of notice that these definitions of the

The world has probably never known an assumption more monstrous than that we are to yield our confidence to those packed conventions of ignorant and brutal men. Out upon the claim, as one of the most insulting and outrageous ever made. It does, indeed, become a humble faith to recognize with reverence a Divine hand in the transmission of Christianity from age to age, and to feel grateful for all that learning and genius have contributed to its defense. But no less is

doctrine of the Trinity are wholly unsatisfactory to the most acute evangelical minds of the present day. It is admitted that they are self-contradictory. The late Professor Moses Stuart, of Andover Theological Seminary, says of them, " They are open to grave and appalling objections." In further criticising their representations he says: "If I understand their views [the Nicene Fathers], they do, in an occult manner indeed, but yet really and effectually interfere with the true equality in substance, power, and glory of the three persons or distinctions in the Godhead. This seems to be taking away with the left hand what we have given with the right. If I say in words that Christ and the Spirit are God, and very God, and yet assign to them attributes or a condition which after all make them *dependent*, and represent them as *derived* and *originated*, then I am in fact no real believer in the doctrine of *true equality* among the persons of the Godhead; or else I use expressions out of their lawful and accustomed sense, and lose myself amid the sound of *words*, while *things* are not examined and defined with scrupulous care and accuracy." Professor Stuart, in *Biblical Repository* for April, 1835.

the obligation to reject with scorn the mass of contradictions and lies which some have tried to foist into the sacred deposit of truth.

When we reflect upon the perversions of Christianity, and upon the divisions and wars among Christians which all these mad passions entailed, one gigantic fact must not be overlooked, though it is not often adduced in this connection.

Of course a great religion, which has acted, and still acts, a tremendous part in history, is the result of many coöperating influences; but who doubts that the vast Mohammedan power found one of the causes of its rise and marvelous diffusion in the doctrinal corruptions and strifes which extended into the centuries that followed the times to which we have here referred? It started as a restorer of the original purity of various religions, Arabian, Jewish, and Christian, but to a large degree it was a protest against the attack upon the unity of God, and the ascription to Jesus of equality with the Supreme Father.

"There is no God but God," was its rallying cry, while both Mohammed and Jesus were regarded as Teachers sent from heaven. We do not comprehend the system of the false Prophet until we look back upon it as in part an offshoot from a corrupt Christianity, — an offshoot which in some fundamental points better preserved the purity of the parent stock, — an offshoot which might have never reached such height and strength had not the errors and passions of Christians opened the way to its growth.

In the next chapter we shall endeavor to prove that the earliest Christian writers, subsequent to the evangelists and apostles, knew nothing of these corruptions.

CHAPTER VII.

THE FATHERS.

JESUS of Nazareth, receiving in conformity with the normal action of his own intellectual and spiritual nature, an inspiration from on high by which he became the Son of God, the Teacher and Guide of humanity, yet born of Mary and Joseph, amid beautiful and touching natural circumstances, which formed part of family memoirs or traditions, not at first noticed, but which were afterwards attached to the gospel histories, and were subsequently misinterpreted in support of a doctrine never heard of in the earliest ages of the Church, but into whose creed it became afterwards incorporated by fraud and violence — if all this be so, we may expect to find traces of it in the writings of the Fathers.

For this purpose it becomes important to give a careful examination to those writings, in the chronological order usually assigned to them, and to note what they have to say about Jesus. If we find in the earliest Christian generations no mention of a supernatural birth, if we see this dogma in after generations first incidentally alluded to, and finally in the fourth and fifth centuries set forth in the manner witnessed in the last chapter, then we may regard these facts as confirmations of the essential truth of the positions here taken.

1. The first Christian writer after the apostles was Clement of Rome. Very little is known of his life. He is claimed as the third successor from St. Peter in the line of Popes; but he lived long before the word Pope had acquired the meaning since so well known. There is a concurrence of all writers in the opinion that he died in Rome, about the year 100, having had some office there as pastor or overseer of the Church, and from thence had sent two epistles to the church at Corinth. The second is short and of little consequence. The first is of considerable length, and of much importance.

Of this epistle Mosheim says, "It is generally, and I think not without reason, considered as indisputably genuine in the main." Neander says, "The first epistle of Clement was in the first centuries read at public worship in many of the churches along with the Scriptures of the New Testament. Although genuine in the main, it is still not exempt from many interpolations." Donaldson, in his "Critical History of Christian Literature and Doctrine," a learned and able work, which we shall have frequent occasion to consult, quotes the evidence of Eusebius and Jerome to prove that it was by them regarded as the trustworthy writing of Clement, and fixes its date as near the close of the first century.

This letter, which is longer than any of the epistles of St. Paul, gives an account of Christ's life and words and promises, and of the leading hopes and duties of believers. It is therefore of value as showing what was the Christian faith and spirit in the very first years after the death of the apostles. We therefore turn to it with interest to mark what it has to say on the subject of the miraculous birth of Christ.

This epistle may be found in the "Apocryphal New Testament," printed in Boston, 1832, and the reader can see for himself that a miraculous conception, or supernatural birth of Jesus, is a point not once named or alluded to. In reading this epistle no one could possibly obtain a hint that such a dogma had ever been taught. It thus follows in the steps of St. Paul, and St. Peter, and St. John, in not recognizing one of the misinterpretations of later ages.

Moreover there is no allusion to the miraculous conception or birth in the other writings of Clement. The weight of this negative evidence, to show that this was not then believed by the Christian Church, will not be overlooked by the reader.

2. Following Clement, the next Christian writer whose works we possess is Polycarp. He was for a long time pastor of a church at Smyrna, from which place he wrote an extant epistle to the Philippians. The date is not far from 150, and though, as Mosheim says, it has been interpolated by weak and superstitious copyists, it is by many considered for the most part genuine and authentic.

Two circumstances give special interest to Polycarp: the first that he had been personally acquainted with the Apostle John; and the second that in his old age he was dragged into the amphitheatre at Smyrna, and required to blaspheme Christ. He said, "Eighty and six years have I served Christ, and he has never done me an injury; how can I blaspheme my King and

Saviour?" Then he was disrobed, bound to a stake, and burned to death.

The epistle to the Philippians is not long. In this, Polycarp writes of Christ as the Son of God, who suffered for us, and whom God raised up from the dead; but there is not the remotest allusion to anything peculiar in his birth. This epistle is also included in the "Apocryphal New Testament," and all can easily procure it and read it for themselves. If the interpretations now put upon the records of Christ's birth were then believed, and were then thought to have the importance now ascribed to them, why did not those early Fathers have one word to say about them?

3. Barnabas is the next Christian writer. He was the companion of St. Paul, and was the noble man who took that apostle by the hand, after his conversion, and when every one beside was still afraid of him. Acts ix. 27. The general epistle which goes by his name is a long letter referring largely to the events of Christ's life and suffering and death, and dwelling upon the fact that he is the Son of God and Saviour of the world. The document is by many regarded as genuine. It is in the "Codex Siniaticus." Origen calls it "a

catholic epistle." Dupin, Dr. Mill, Archbishop Wake, and others admit its authenticity; but, on the other hand, Neander and Donaldson think it has no claim to be considered authentic. Mosheim's opinion is that it was written by a man called Barnabas, "not wanting in piety, but of a weak and superstitious character," and "the early Christians, led away by a name for which they entertained the highest reverence, attributed it to the friend and companion of St. Paul."

Whether genuine or not, one thing is certain, it makes no allusion to anything unusual in the birth of Jesus, as any one may see for himself, since this also is included in the "Apocryphal New Testament," before referred to.

4. The Shepherd of Hermas is the next Christian writer. His extant works are divided into three books, "Visions," "Commands," and "Similitudes." There is a great diversity of opinion as to the character of these works, and the time and place of their composition. Some think the writer is the Hermas referred to by St. Paul. Romans xvi. 14. Others suppose he was a brother of Pius I. Bishop of Rome in 154, and that he lived and wrote in Italy. Mosheim doubts if the writer was sane. Neander says his works were

in high repute, in the second century. Origen often quotes them, as did Eusebius and Athanasius. Donaldson regards them as very interesting; and to those who call them silly, he says that Bunyan's Pilgrim's Progress would have seemed absurd to Latin critics. He adds that Bunsen compares them to Dante's "Divina Commedia."[1]

[1] But it should be added that Bunsen compares them only in certain points, which he names as follows: "It is very remarkable that Hermas has performed his task with the same religious respect for the historical individuality of his person that Dante exhibits nearly twelve centuries later; and moreover, we do not scruple to say, reveals not only an equal intensity of religious belief, but a far greater hopefulness for the future; therefore really a much stronger faith in the victory of the true world-transforming Christianity than was possessed by the great mediæval Florentine. Both present us with a picture of the inward history of the soul, of its awakening from selfishness, and the mad pursuit of sensual pleasure, to faith in the Divine redeeming love, and of the passage through a purifying state of suffering to the blessedness of peace; both depict these changes as taking place after the close of the earthly life. But while the prophet of the Middle Ages nowhere expresses any hope for the earthly life of Christendom, for the existing ecclesiastical form of God's kingdom, but, on the contrary, transfers all blessedness and all just retribution to the future world, Hermas, in the very midst of persecution, nay, on the eve of a new persecution which he sees to be impending, with the eye of his spirit gazes with rapture on the magnificent expansion of the kingdom of

In bulk they make a quarter part of the "Apocryphal New Testament." They refer to the leading events of Christ's life, death, and resurrection; but throughout the whole there is no hint of anything extraordinary in his birth. Donaldson says, "The writer's views in regard to Christ are especially Ebionistic."

In coming down now to the early part of the second half of the second century, we meet with five Christian writers who were nearly contemporaries, — Hegesippus, Athenagoras, Theophilus, Tatian, and Justin Martyr. We will give a glance at each in the order in which we have here named them.

5. Hegesippus was a converted Jew, who visited Corinth and Rome about the year 170. He wrote the history of ecclesiastical affairs from the death of Christ to his own time; but nothing of it remains except some scattered fragments, from which it appears that it was a book of notes, recollections, and scraps of information. Donaldson says he speaks of Christ as the Son of God, and this is about all the doctrinal information we get from him. There is no reference whatever to a supposed miraculous birth.

God that was destined to replace the moribund vitality of the Greek and Roman world."— *God in History*, vol. iii., p. 83.

6. Athenagoras was of Alexandria, and was a leader of a school there. He became a Christian, and published a defense of the Christians about the year 168. Two works of his are extant, the defense above alluded to, and a small treatise on the resurrection. Critics speak of him as writing in a clear and strong style, and pronounce his defense of the Christians the best produced in that age. He gives a full account of the Christian system, and dwells particularly upon its power to purify and ennoble the conduct of man. Following the style of the Gnostic writers he calls the Logos the reason of God, but he has nothing to say about a supernatural birth of Jesus.

7. Theophilus was of Antioch. Eusebius says he was the sixth overseer of the church in that city. The only extant work of his is addressed to Autolycus, designed to show the falsity of heathenism, and the truth of Christianity. For this purpose he cites the chief doctrines and precepts of the Gospels; but there is no allusion to anything miraculous in the birth of Christ.

8. Tatian, a Syrian, brought up a heathen, was a traveling lecturer, but became converted to Christianity, and is chiefly remarkable for his leaning towards Gnosticism and asceticism. He

left several works, only one of which is extant — an Oration to the Greeks, commended by Eusebius and Origen. His object is to show that there is much in what the Greeks call barbarian religions which is worthy of their notice. He denounces the Greek mythology, and holds up for imitation the pure morals of the Christians. He regards the Logos as the power of reason, emanating from God as a light emanates from a burning torch; but he gives no account of the birth of Christ as differing from the birth of others.

9. Justin Martyr was born at Neapolis, near Sichem, in Samaria, about the beginning of the second century. He is supposed to have been of Roman descent, at any rate was not a Jew by birth. He devoted himself to the study of the prevailing systems of philosophy, — the Stoic, the Pythagorean, the Platonic, — but none of them satisfied him. One day as he was walking near the sea shore — we are not told what shore — he met an old man of gentle and venerable appearance who talked with him about the object of life, the existence of God, the soul of man; and finally called his attention to the Hebrew prophets, through whom the gates of light might be opened to him, and God and Christ might give

him understanding. It may have been one who had himself personally seen Jesus. "And suddenly," said Justin, "a fire was lighted in my soul, and I was possessed with a love of the prophets, and of those men who are Christ's friends."

We know little of the events of Justin's life, and the most important thing that we know is that he published a defense of Christians addressed to Antoninus Pius, another work of a similar kind addressed to Marcus Aurelius, a Dialogue with Trypho, the Jew, and a few other works of less value. They mark him as one of the most important of the early Christian writers. Such was the result of that chance conversation by the sea-shore.

He is regarded as a man of good culture and extensive reading, but not a profound thinker, nor a systematic reasoner. He was not a theologian, nor an ecclesiastic, but rather a philosopher; and he wore the mantle of a philosopher as long as he lived. He wins our love by his bold and manly address to the Roman Emperor, to whom he writes, "We can receive no injury from you unless we are workers of iniquity. You can kill us; injure us you cannot."

He conceived of Christ as the chief angel of

God, the Logos-agent of the Almighty, whose offices are recorded throughout the Old Testament history. He refers to the events of Christ's life as we find them recorded in the Gospels. He is the first writer, we believe, who describes Christ as not born of human parents. He believed that the Logos of God, which in the Old Testament ages had assumed so many forms, might in these latter times come in the form of man without human seed; and this, as he says, was exactly parallel to what, as the Grecians taught, had happened to many sons of Jupiter.

Yet this view of Christ's birth is a point to which he refers only incidentally, without assigning any great importance to it; the reason of which is obvious, for he adds, "Some of my friends, of our Christian sect, ἀπὸ τοῦ ἡμετέρου γένους, maintain that Christ was born of human parents;" and in another place, in a list of heretics, he did not include the Ebionites, who never believed the miraculous birth.

Here, then, is the first suggestion of anything miraculous in the birth of Christ. It first appears nearly two centuries after his birth; and here no prominence is assigned to it, and it is coupled with the distinct admission that some did not believe it. What is equally surprising is, that for his own faith in Christ's supernatural birth Justin appeals to no testimony or traditions which must have existed at his time, had the event occurred or been generally believed; but finds an argument for it in the heathen genealogies of the gods. It is to be added, that Justin did not know the Hebrew language, and perhaps was not therefore able to appreciate the linguistic reasons which had kept the apostles and fathers before him from assigning to the stories in St. Luke the sense which he attached to them.

We have made a study of succeeding Fathers of the Church, such as Cyprian, Tertullian, Origen, with a view of bringing forward the statements of their belief concerning the birth of Jesus. But to extend our examination of their writings any farther would be giving a disproportionate attention to this point; nor is it really necessary, since the remark in general terms is sufficient that, subsequent to the point of time to which we have now arrived, allusions to a supposed miraculous birth of Christ are found more or less distinctly in nearly all Christian writers. The prominence that was now given to this dogma, through the causes adverted to in our fifth chapter; the new style of language in regard to it that now came into fashion; and the multitudinous speculations and absurd exegesis to which it gave rise, will be sufficiently apparent by a glance, which we propose to give in the next chapter, at the modes of patristic reasoning.

CHAPTER VIII.

PATRISTIC REASONING.

IN the above review of the writings of the earliest Fathers, we have seen that there was no allusion to the miraculous birth of Christ in the extant works of those authors who immediately succeeded the apostles. It is only when we come down to the latter part of the second century that we find the first traces of that dogma.

It may be of some service to place directly under the eye a synopsis of the results we have thus far reached.

St. Matthew and St. Luke have annexed to their Gospels some detached family traditions, to which were ascribed but little importance, as these contained merely private reminiscences of the birth of Jesus.

St. Mark and St. John do not record them at all.

The sermons of the first preachers of the Gospel, reported so fully in the Acts of the Apostles, make no mention of them.

The Epistles of St. Paul, and St. Peter, and St. John do not relate them.

Clemens Romanus, the first Christian writer after the apostles, is silent in regard to any thing supernatural in the birth of Christ.

To him succeeded Polycarp, who is equally silent.

Barnabas, a companion, as is supposed, of St. Paul, is the next Christian writer, and he does not refer to it.

The same remark is to be made of the Shepherd of Hermas.

Then come Hegesippus, the Church historian, and Athenagoras of Alexandria, and Theophilus of Antioch, and Tatian the Syrian, who are all equally silent on this point.

Justin Martyr, in the second century, is the first writer who speaks of something miraculous in the birth of Christ, to which view he seems to have been led by his heathen training, as such a birth was similar to what had happened to sons of Jupiter; but he assigns no prominence to this point, and says expressly that some Christians did not believe it.

To show that in the first generations of Christians this dogma of a miraculous conception was unknown, there is a still more important proof to be now submitted, and a proof which must be regarded as decisive.

Its early absence is distinctly and expressly admitted by those who began to broach it and maintain it; and they assigned special reasons why it had not before been received.

The facts of the case were as follows: When Christian preachers and writers first began to attach so much importance to the records of Christ's birth, surprise was naturally awakened; and they were told to look to the traditions of the Church, for it was well known that these supernatural interpretations were of recent origin, and were unknown to the first Christian believers.

How was this objection met? It was admitted that the real facts about Christ's birth had not before been understood, and reasons were given why they had been lately discovered. If we find these reasons to be very weak and absurd, they are none the less interesting in view of the point which we have here in mind.

And now what are these reasons?

If our readers have ever turned over the leaves of the writings of the Fathers, some of them now quite accessible in the beautiful English "Ante-Nicene Library of the Fathers," they will be prepared for the strange mixture of a sincere, earnest faith, with feeble puerilities, and foolish fancies, and solemn absurdities, which there abound. We may begin our citations with almost any one, and we will turn first to no obscure name, to St. Chrysostom — him of the golden mouth.

In reference to the miraculous birth he observes : " This was concealed and managed as a great and wonderful thing to preserve the Virgin, and cover her from wicked suspicions. For if this had been known to the Jews from the beginning, they would have stoned the Virgin, abusing her for what would have been said, and have condemned her for adultery. . . . . Nor did the Virgin herself dare to confess this. For observe how she calls Joseph the father of Jesus, when she said to him, ' Behold thy father and I have sought thee.' If the truth had been suspected, Jesus would not have been thought to have been the son of David; and this not being admitted, many mischiefs would have arisen. On the same account the angels did not mention this except to Mary and Joseph only, but not to the shepherds, though they acquainted them with the fact of the birth."

But St. Chrysostom does not tell us by what means the full facts became known two or three hundred years after the event. It could not have been from the narratives of Matthew and Luke, for these had long been read without deriving from them the dogma in question. Was there any special revelation in later times? Or how did the "management" that shut out the mischiefs, and screened the Virgin, and taught her to prevaricate, unfold the knowledge of the case to St. Chrysostom?

Of course it occurred to many to ask, If Mary was the only parent of Jesus, why was she married at all? Had there been no marriage, the presumption of her virginity, and the exclusion of any paternity, would have been more probable. But answers were at hand.

St. Jerome gives three reasons why Mary was married to Joseph. 1. That it might appear that Jesus was descended from David. 2. Lest Mary should have been stoned as an adulteress. 3. That she might have a guardian in the flight into Egypt.

St. Basil and Theophylact take a still higher flight in accounting for Mary's marriage. St. Basil says, "Mary was married to Joseph that the devil might not suspect that she was a virgin, for he knew that Christ was to be born of a virgin." In the same strain argues Theophylact, who says, "Mary was married that she by this means might deceive the devil. For the devil, having heard that Christ was to be born of a virgin, observed the virgins. She therefore married Joseph to deceive the deceiver."

Following in this same strain, Damascenes says, "The virginity of Mary, her delivery, and the birth of Christ, were all concealed from the devil."

It was all plain to St. Ambrose why Jesus himself never alluded to the miraculous conception, for that writer says, "Our Lord rather chose that his origin should be unknown than that his mother's chastity should be questioned." The fact of his divine origin was quite subordinate to a false opinion about his mother.

Curious, too, is it to see how many *a priori* reasons the Fathers had for the birth of Christ from a virgin. In that age they all knew exactly how it ought to take place. Cyril of Alexandria, the same whose contest with Nestorius we have described in a former chapter, said: "Christ ought to have such a birth that his presence and manifestation to the world might have something in it worthy of a God."

Lactantius said that as God was without father and mother, so the son had to be born twice, that he might be born without father and mother; for he was first spiritually generated by God the Father only, and so without mother; and then again he was carnally born by the Virgin alone, and so without father.

St. Augustine thought that the salvation of the female sex was particularly intended by Christ being born of a woman only; for as he was derived solely from a woman, he would naturally feel a deeper interest in woman's lot; while if he had had a father as well as a mother, he might have taken more than a due care of the male sex. Such was St. Augustine's reasoning.

St. Irenæus asks, If Christ were born of Joseph, how could he have surpassed Solomon or David? Were he produced in the same manner, and their descendant, Omnipotence could have made nothing more of him than of them.

Justin Martyr said that Christ was born of a virgin, that by the same means that disobedience came by a word, that is of the serpent, by the same means it should be terminated by a word.

For Eve, a virgin, uncorrupt, conceived by the word of the serpent, and brought forth death; so the Virgin Mary conceived by the word of the angel, and brought forth deliverance from death.

The same conceit was taken up by others. Cyril of Jerusalem said that "as death came by the virgin Eve, so it was necessary that life should be brought by a virgin." But St. Ambrose varied the comparison, for he said, "Adam was made of the virgin earth, and Christ was made from a virgin woman."

St. Chrysostom knew exactly what sort of a birth it was fitting Jesus should have, for he said, "It is not because marriage is a bad thing, but because virginity is better; and it behooved the Lord of all to have a more splendid entrance into the world than ours, for it was the entrance of a king. He ought to be born of a woman in common with us; but to be born without marriage which makes him greater than us."

St. Athanasius also dwells on this thought that Christ's birth makes him greater than all, for his eloquence flames out as follows: "What righteous person, what holy prophet or patriarch in all the sacred writings, was born of a virgin only? or what woman was sufficient for the conception of a man without a man?"

This opinion, that it was specially honorable to Jesus to be without a father, is frequently presented in these writings, as if what we think is honorable is to decide our view of what God has done. We might think it more honorable still if Jesus had had no mother, had not been born at all, or not born an infant, or not born in a stable; and it is not easy to see where such human ideas of what is honorable might stop.

The Emperor Constantine, in his oration before the Council of Nice, says, "When Christ was to live among men he invented a new way of being born; for there was a conception without a marriage, a delivery of a pure virgin, and a young woman was the Mother of God." This idea of inventing a new way of birth has been reproduced in recent times.[1]

In reviewing the above citations, perhaps no one can read them without seeing that we here meet many expressions wholly different from anything found in the writings of the apostles and of their first successors. The entire body of the

[1] See *Disquisitions and Notes on the Gospel of Matthew.* By John H. Morison, Boston, 1860, p. 37.

literature of these last named writers does not offer so much about the birth of Christ as we may find on one page of the writings of the third and fourth centuries. The strata of thought is as abruptly different as any strata of gravel and clay or granite and trap the geologist knows.

The allegorical mode of interpretation which so much flourished in that age opened a wide door for the loss of any sound practical sense, and for the entrance of any improbable conceit. It is important to mark the fact, that this mode came into vogue among those who were out of the circle of the strongest Jewish influence, and were in contact with Greek civilization. Hence they were not hampered by Hebrew lexicography or traditions. It was the idea of Origen that every passage of Scripture had a spiritual element, and sometimes, as he maintained, a spiritual truth in a corporeal falsehood. With such latitude of interpretation, how many prophecies and hints of the miraculous birth of Christ might be found!

We read in Psalm cxxxix. 16, " In thy book all my members were written." Epiphanius thought that David said this in the name of Christ, and the book was the Virgin's womb. In the Song of Solomon iv. 12, we read, " A garden enclosed is my sister, my spouse, a spring shut up, a fountain sealed." This was often referred to the Virgin; and the visitor to Rome may see this text cited on the tasteless monument in the Piazza di Spagna, erected in honor of the dogma of the Immaculate Conception. In Psalm cxxxix. 13, we read, " Thou hast covered me in my mother's womb." Eusebius applies this to Christ, whose miraculous conception was hid from the world.

In the very first verse of Genesis a prediction of the Virgin Mary was found. " In the beginning God created the heaven and the earth." That means Joachim and Anna, the father and mother of the Virgin. " And the earth was without form and void." That is, Anna was barren. " And darkness was on the face of the deep." This is the sorrow she felt. "And the spirit of God moved upon the face of the waters." That is, the Holy Ghost giving conception to Anna. " And God said, let there be light." That is, the Virgin was born.

Probably it is such exegesis as this that led the poet to say: —

> "The fly-blown text conceives an alien brood,
> And turns to maggots what was meant for food."

It may be that we have now seen enough of

the Fathers to lead us to indorse the opinion of Milton, who says: "Whatsoever time or the heedless hand of blind chance hath drawn from of old to this present, in her huge drag-net, whether fish or sea-weed, shells or shrubs, unpicked, unchosen, — these are the Fathers. Seeing, therefore, some men deeply conversant in books have had so little care of late to give the world a better account of their reading, than by divulging needless tractates stuffed with the specious names of Ignatius and Polycarp, with fragments of old mythologies and legends to distract and stagger the multitude of credulous readers, and mislead them from their strong guards and places of safety under the tuition of Holy Writ, it came into my thoughts to persuade myself, setting all distances and nice respects aside, that I could do religion and my country no better service for the time, than by doing my utmost endeavor to recall the people of God from this vain foraging after straw, and to reduce them to their firm stations under the standard of the Gospel, by making appear to them, first the insufficiency, next the inconveniency, and lastly the impiety of these gay testimonies that their great doctors would bring them to dote on."[1]

[1] Milton's *Prelatical Episcopacy*.

We are apt to suppose that the fact of their nearness to the times of the apostles gives the Fathers an authority superior to all other writers. We forget, as Macaulay has well said, "that their disadvantages in other respects place them below a third rate student of Scripture of a later age, just as a man with bad eyes may not see an object so clearly at fifty yards, as another with good eyes may see it at half a mile. Almost all the Fathers had very bad eyes, and they attempted to remedy the defect with worse spectacles."

That among such men there should gradually grow up a misinterpretation of the records of the birth of Jesus, and an assignment to them of an importance not at first thought of, will seem all the more probable if we remember two facts which marked the primitive age of Christianity.

The first is that some time elapsed before the writings of the New Testament were reverenced as a part of the Holy Scriptures. Those writings were not composed during the generation that was contemporary with Jesus. Even after they had been gathered into the form in which we now have them, converts from Judaism could not at once have held them in the same light in which they regarded their older sacred books.

Of course the life of Jesus was of deep interest to them. Yet it was not the subject of the critical study elsewhere bestowed. Of this we have plenary proof. Among the immense mass of extant writings of the Fathers, it is surprising to mark what a vast proportion is commentary on the Old Testament. We see the cause of this only when we reflect how slowly the reverence for that book would be shared by works which must have seemed so modern. There was a constant attempt to prove that Christ was foretold and described in the Law, the Prophets, and the Psalms, — the same tendency so manifest in the evangelists, who pored over the Jewish Scriptures to find predictions of events in the life of Jesus. It is probable, judging from the titles of books that have come down to us, that in the first years of the Gospels The Song of Solomon received more critical study than the Gospels themselves. Origen, between A. D. 215 and 254, gave twenty-eight years of his life, terminated at this last date, to a critical study of the Old Testament, bringing to the task vast learning, and unexampled boldness and acuteness of speculation, while he bestowed comparatively little attention upon that New Testament which, as he seems not to have suspected, would soon eclipse in interest the elder Scriptures. We need not say how favorable all this was to the creeping in of wide-spread misconceptions of the real meaning of the Gospels.

But, secondly, what critical study there was among the first generations of believers was not only devoid of any scientific accuracy, but was worthless through false rules of interpretation. The reader of the preceding pages has seen evidence enough of the love of allegory, and the search for mystical but baseless meanings. Men then applied to the words of the evangelical narrative " not an historical criticism, but abstruse metaphysical conceptions. . . . . The world and society presented conditions less and less favorable to sane criticism. It was under these conditions that the dogma now called orthodox grew up." [1]

Thus an age of puerile speculations still further favored the rise of the misconceptions on which we have dwelt, and which in time acquired the dogmatic form set forth in the "Apostles' Creed," so called, to the history and meaning of which the next chapter will be devoted.

[1] *Literature and Dogma*, pp. 276, 282, by Matthew Arnold.

CHAPTER IX.

THE APOSTLES' CREED.

IT may be thought that the expressions in the "Apostles' Creed," "Conceived of the Holy Ghost, born of the Virgin Mary," refute the leading idea of this book; and it becomes necessary therefore to notice this symbol of faith. An account of its origin may be found in various ecclesiastical histories, and several distinct treatises have unfolded its history and explained its meaning. The well-known and approved work in English, by Sir Peter King, has long been before the public; and a more extended and thorough publication in French has lately appeared, entitled "Le Symbole des Apôtres," by Michel Nicolas, Paris, 1867.

It will occur to every one that there is no allusion to this Creed in the sermons or epistles of the first preachers of Christianity, nor is it named by any writer in the earliest ages of the Church. Had it been the work of the apostles, it would often have been appealed to in the sharp controversies of those times ; nor is this negative evidence the only proof that it was composed in a later day.

Not till the end of the third century do we meet with any reference to this Creed as having the authority of the apostles. Of course, some of the articles it embraces had been frequently named before as matters of belief. When Philip baptized the Eunuch, Acts viii. 37, the latter said, " I believe that Jesus Christ is the Son of God." This was all the creed the apostle required. To that simple profession of faith point after point was afterward added, as we shall soon see; but not till about three hundred years afterwards were all these points brought together in a form that claimed apostolic authority.

The truth is this Creed is in the main of Roman Catholic manufacture. The Greek Church never has acknowledged it. Luther said it had no more authority than the symbol of St. Ambrose or St. Augustine. Calvin thought its origin so late and its author so uncertain that it had no special value. Zwingle believed there was no copy of it prior to the fourth century. Sir Peter King says, " Part of this Creed was transmitted down from the apostles, and other parts were afterwards added by the governors of the church to prevent heresies." He says also that the first Christians had a variety of symbols of faith, which were not usually committed to writing, but were transmitted orally with some feeling of secrecy and awe, and were taught to the baptized; but the profession of faith did not take the form in which we have it in the Apostles' Creed till centuries after Christ.

The French author we have referred to is entirely in accord with all this, and says that no creed under the name of the apostles can be found earlier than the fourth century, and adds that St. Ambrose, Bishop of Milan, is the first writer who calls a creed by this name; that it was in Italy that this name was first generally used; that the Church in the East long after this did not receive this Creed, while the Greek Church, as we have before said, does not to this day own it.

It will be more interesting to show how, according both to Sir Peter King and M. Nicolas, the different articles of this Creed came to find their place; and this point will shed still further light upon the time of its origin. So far from being completed at once, it received additions generation after generation, to guard against successive heresies. *Crescit eundo*, and this is the reason why it exceeded in length the true Apostles' Creed of Philip and the Eunuch.

Thus the Creed was made to read, "I believe in *one* God," not only in opposition to pagan polytheism, but, as King shows, against some heretical Christians, who, in the third and fourth centuries taught that there were two coeval and independent principles; while others propagated opinions which bordered on tritheism. The approved faith was in *one* God only.

It was said "Maker of Heaven and Earth," because the Gnostic heresy of the early centuries taught that matter was not created by God, but was the work of some being at war with him, or inferior to him. Matter was believed to be the source of all impurity, and could not come therefore from the hands of an infinitely holy God. But the true doctrine was that God made the earth as well as the heaven.

Nicolas says that the expression, "In Jesus Christ *our Lord*," was aimed against those who held that a multitude of eons emanated from God, to whom allegiance was due. This article affirmed Jesus to be the sole revealer of God, and Master of Christians.

The phrase, "conceived by the Holy Ghost," was inserted, as both King and Nicolas show, to oppose the opinions of the Ebionites, and the Judaizing Christians, who believed that Jesus was a son of Joseph as well as of Mary. The next phrase in the Creed, " born of the Virgin Mary," was directed against those who held that Jesus had a corporeal existence only in appearance; that his body was a mere phantom; had no substance derived from his mother. It was out of the controversies of the third century, that this part of the Creed was shaped; and here is another proof of its late formation.

"Suffered under Pontius Pilate;" this was placed in the Creed because there were some in the second century who taught that Christ's body was incapable of suffering. " Crucified, dead, and buried ;" Nicolas says these expressions are a literal repetition of the frequent declarations of Ignatius, Irenæus, Tertullian, and Origen against the Docetæ.

"He descended into Hell." By this last word was denoted Hades, the place where it was supposed all departed spirits were confined prior to the final judgment. Hence in the parable both Lazarus and Dives are represented as being there. There had been from the first some vague idea that the human soul of Jesus visited that place between the time of his death and his resurrection. To this it is supposed St. Peter alludes, 1 Peter iii. 19: "Went and preached to the spirits in prison." No prominence was given to this point till in subsequent centuries it connected itself with two important articles of faith: the first, that Jesus had a human soul, in opposition to those who denied his perfect humanity; and the second, that Jesus went to the place of departed spirits, which was Purgatory, to carry his redeeming work there.

In our times probably the general opinion attached to the sentence, " He descended into Hell," is that *he died;* and the Episcopal Church does not impose any interpretation of this phrase. But at the time the Creed was formed, in this point there was something more meant than a mere tautology. King gives the chief prominence to the supposition that it was inserted against those who thought Christ did not have a human soul; that the Logos took its place.

From this opinion Nicolas dissents. He says

that it could not have been admitted that the mere human soul of Christ could carry on the work of redemption in the place of departed spirits; and besides, it was held by the Fathers that the Divine nature accompanied Christ to that place. He therefore sees in this expression the recognition of a middle place between earth and heaven, Purgatory, where the Saviour went to redeem the pious souls who had died in the Old Testament ages. Nicolas shows that the belief in Purgatory took a fresh life from this part of the Creed, and has been attached to it ever since.

A like inference may be drawn from the expression in the Creed, "The Communion of Saints." Protestants see in that clause only a recognition of a common feeling among all devout men. But Nicolas shows that this is by no means the idea which presided at its formation, and which has been in all past ages attached to it. It sets forth, he says, the fact of a unity among all redeemed souls, on earth or in heaven; and it is used chiefly to justify the invocation of angels and saints, and the very life-blood of the clause is found in this idea.

Looking at the Creed as a whole we see at

once, from its disproportions, that it took its shape controversially. Regarded as a full Christian Creed it is singularly deficient. Nothing is said about the offices, ministrations, and comforts of the Holy Spirit. The great subject of God the Father is dismissed in a line or two; while controverted points about Christ are brought forward at greater length. After all, many of the important verities of the Christian faith find no statement whatever. It is more a polemic weapon than an enumeration of the truths which lie deepest in the believer's heart.

Bunsen, in his book entitled, "God in History," vol. iii. p. 55, says, "The most ancient formula of the Apostles' Creed for which we have documentary evidence is that used in the church of Alexandria, A. D. 200, the whole of which, word for word, is as follows: —

"I believe in the only true God, the Father Almighty; and in his only begotten Son, Jesus Christ, our Lord and Saviour;

"And in the Holy Ghost, the Giver of life."

The same writer adds: "It was not until the fifth century that the confession of faith used in public worship, entitled 'The Apostles' Creed,' grew out of the gradual expansion of this earlier baptismal formula."

Nicolas gives many versions of this Creed in the early centuries before it took the final shape in which we commonly see it, and then says: —

"Rien ne me semble plus propre à donner une idée exacte au long travail auquel le Crédo a été soumis avant d'arriver à sa forme définitive, que les remaniements successifs de cet article, remaniements dont il n'est pas très-difficile de suivre presque pas à pas la série. Les mentionner c'est prouver que notre formulaire a été l'œuvre de plusieurs siècles." Page 86.

Thus we see that this Creed can rightly be called the Apostles' Creed only in that general sense in which the college of cardinals is called the Apostolic College, or a papal ambassador is called an Apostolic Nuncio. It is hardly worth while to state how much Roman Catholic tradition has glorified the formation of this document, representing that, before the apostles left Jerusalem, the twelve came together, and each one contributed a sentence, as follows: —

Peter, I believe in God the Father Almighty;
John, Maker of Heaven and Earth;

THE APOSTLES' CREED. 163

James, And in Jesus Christ, his only Son, our Lord;

Andrew, Conceived of the Holy Ghost, born of the Virgin Mary;

Philip, Suffered under Pontius Pilate, was crucified, dead, and buried;

Thomas, Descended to hell, the third day he rose from the dead;

Bartholomew, He ascended to Heaven, he is seated at the right hand of God the Father Almighty;

Matthew, From thence he shall come to judge the quick and the dead;

James the Less, I believe in the Holy Ghost, the Holy Catholic Church;

Simeon, The Communion of Saints, the forgiveness of sins;

Jude, The resurrection of the body;

Matthias, The life everlasting.[1]

The assignment of sentences to the apostles has been variously made. There is an old Latin poem, attributed to Saint Bernard, which gives a

---

[1] We see that Mr. Longfellow has appended the Apostles' Creed, with this assignment, to his *Divine Tragedy*. The fiction of the assignment is not without some interest for its antiquity, but it was a fraud perpetrated centuries after the apostolic age.

different distribution, and is in itself of some interest. Perhaps the omission in it of the miraculous conception was only through some metrical necessity.

> Articuli fidei sunt bis sex corde tenendi,
> Quos Christi socii docuerunt, pneumati pleni:
> Credo Deum Patrem, *Petrus* inquit, cuncta creatum;
> *Andreas* dixit, Ego credo Jesum fore Christum;
> Conceptum, natum, *Jacobus;* passumque, *Joannes;*
> Infera, *Philippus,* fugit; *Thomas* que, revixit;
> Scendit, *Bartholomeus;* veniet censore, *Matthæus;*
> Pneuma, *Minor Jacobus; Simon,* peccata remittet;
> Restituit, *Judas,* carnem; vitamque, *Matthias.*

We need not repeat that this picnic origin, as one has called it, is a late invention.

We close this review by marking the fact that the first skeletons of the Apostles' Creed do not state a belief of anything miraculous in the birth of Christ. We have seen that the earliest Alexandrian version, quoted above from Bunsen, has no clause of this kind. Such is the fact also of a sketch of a summary of Christian truths, somewhat resembling the Apostles' Creed, found in the writings of Ignatius. It speaks of faith in "Jesus Christ, who is of the race of David, Son of Mary, who was veritably born, has eaten and drunk, who has truly suffered persecution under Pontius Pilate, has been veritably crucified and was dead, in the view of all who are in heaven, upon the earth, and under the earth, who has truly arisen from the dead, his father having raised him up as He will raise us up." [1]

It will be observed that here is a statement of that simpler, earlier faith on the subject of the birth of Jesus, which, as we have seen, was all that the Christians of the first ages professed; and in a creed that has grown up as has the Apostles' Creed no statement it contains can be brought as an argument for or against the faith of the first disciples of Christ.

In support of the general thesis of this book there is another subject which merits notice. It is the worship of the Virgin Mary, — a worship which grew up contemporaneously with the ascription to Jesus of a supernatural origin. The next chapter will cast an important side-light on the point under discussion.

[1] *Le Symbole des Apôtres*, p. 13.

CHAPTER X.

MARIOLATRY.

THE adoration of the Mother of Jesus is one of the consequences of the misinterpretation of the records of his birth; and in Roman Catholic countries her image has taken a hold upon the imagination and affections, which arrests our attention and merits consideration.

"It is remarkable," says Lecky, in his "History of Morals," "that the Jews, who of the three great nations of antiquity certainly produced in history and poetry the smallest number of illustrious women, should have furnished the world with its supreme female ideal; and it is also a striking illustration of the qualities which prove most attractive in woman, that one of whom we know nothing except her gentleness and her sorrow, should have exercised a magnetic power upon the world, incomparably greater than was exercised by the most majestic female patriots of Paganism." Vol. ii., p. 389.

MARIOLATRY. 167

Archbishop Whately, in tracing the errors of Romanism to some principles in human nature, might readily have discerned in this worship of the Virgin something which made it fondly welcome to the heart. Where the idea of God was thrown into a mysterious and awful background, and the court of heaven was painted by the imagination after the fashion of an earthly court of the Middle Ages, and access to the monarch was with difficulty obtained, and only abject fear and trembling could be felt in his presence, with what joy was received the dogma of a gentle and loving one to go between the suppliant and that King of kings, — one who had all womanly tenderness and pity, into whose ear every sorrow and wish might be poured, and whose influence was all powerful in heaven.

Her image was set up everywhere, and in Catholic Europe may still be seen, not only in lofty cathedrals, and venerated parish churches, and sacred retreats for the dead, but in the corners of the streets, in shrines by the wayside, in resting places of the mountain paths, on the inclosures of the vineyards, over the doors of the houses, on the walls of the humblest dwelling, in the shop of the artisan ; and she of the loving smile, with the infant Jesus in her arms, seen by every one, from the first memory of youth to the last look in death, became a real being whose existence, and compassion, and power it was impossible to doubt. God occupied no place in their hearts compared with that of Mary.[1]

Of course all this was founded on false conceptions of God. Mariolatry could never have existed had men believed what Jesus had taught of the Father, who clothes the lilies with their beauty, numbers the hairs of our head, and without whose notice not even a sparrow falls to the ground. It is the grand distinction of that Divine Teacher to present to us in God a being whom the heart may love, whom it may approach in confidence and joy, and before whom it may pour out all its cares, "for he careth for us." But when a false religion has shrouded the throne of the Almighty with awful mystery and terror, the human heart will make some object to love, for to love is one of the necessities of our nature.

---

[1] The lines of Wordsworth to the Virgin may here be recalled: —

"Thy very name, O Lady, flings
O'er blooming fields and gushing springs
A tender sense of shadowy fear,
And chastening sympathies."

There has been much speculation as to the effect in Roman Catholic countries of the worship of the Virgin; and it has often been said that it has elevated the position of woman. We think that such an opinion could not have been founded on anything the traveler now sees in those countries. The position of woman in Protestant lands is beyond comparison higher. But after all this is not decisive. No one can tell how much lower woman might have fallen had she not been shielded by some associations of infinite purity and holiness with her to whom so many prayers have been addressed; and this refuge in all times of sorrow and peril to one who was believed to be full of gentleness and love, how could it wholly fail to do much to soften rugged natures, and to teach sweet lessons of pity and forgiveness?

Probably the homage given to the Virgin Mary would have had a more humanizing influence, and would have done more to elevate her sex, had not superstition placed her on a pinnacle so far above all other women. Her birth was regarded as miraculous, for the supposed law of transmitted sin was suspended in the case of her who was the Queen of Heaven, and the Mother of God; and this accumulation around her of supernatural attributes, how did it make all others of her sex appear in comparison? Her beauty, purity, gentleness, and love were something more than human, and therefore were no example and measure for others, who perhaps were sometimes even scorned by the contrast. Who can doubt that both Jesus and his mother will have a profounder influence over human hearts, the closer they are brought to our humanity?

To show what influence she has had in past ages the old legends of the church have a special interest. The "Lives of the Saints" are full of stories, many of them wild and absurd, but some of them singularly beautiful and suggestive of the intercessions and helps of the Virgin; and we quite agree with what a late writer says, who expresses himself as follows: —

"There is, if I mistake not, no department of literature the importance of which is more inadequately realized than the "Lives of the Saints." Even when they have no direct historical value, they have a moral value of the very highest order. They may not tell us with accuracy what men did at particular epochs, but they display with the utmost vividness what men thought and felt, their measure of probability, and their ideal of excellence. Decrees of councils, elaborate treatises of theologians, creeds, liturgies, and canons, are only the husks of religious history. They reveal what was professed and argued before the world, but not that which was realized in the imagination and enshrined in the heart. The history of art, which in its ruder day reflected with delicate fidelity the fleeting images of an anthropomorphic age, is in this respect invaluable; but still more important is that vast Christian mythology which grew up spontaneously from the intellectual condition of the time, included all its dearest hopes, wishes, ideals, and imaginings, and constituted during many centuries the popular literature of Christendom."[1]

No English writer, we believe, has looked into this mythology so much as Mrs. Jameson, and her delightful works on the old church legends are an invaluable companion to the visitor of the galleries of Europe. Alban Butler's "Lives of the Saints" is another storehouse; but a work in Italian, the "Golden Legend," by Giacobo Voragine, is the most famous collection, — a fine copy of which, now rarely obtained, fortunately rewarded our search in an old bookstore in Flor-

[1] Lecky's *History of Morals*, vol. ii., p. 119.

ence. Later than this a French publication, entitled "Apparitions et Révélations de la Très-Sainte Vierge," by Paul Sausseret, gives us in two volumes one hundred and forty legends of the Virgin.

In casting one's eye over this vast mass of mediæval literature, the first thing that one observes is that these legends cover the entire course of the Virgin's history, — her Birth, her Presentation in the Temple, her Espousal, her Marriage, her Conception, the Birth of her Son, the Visit of the Magi, the Purification, the Flight into Egypt, the Repose in Egypt, the Seeking of Jesus amid the Doctors of the Temple, the Marriage at Cana of Galilee, Mary at the Crucifixion, the Stabat Mater,[1] Mary at the Descent from the Cross, Mary at the Entombment, Mary at the Resurrection, her Death, her Ascension, her Assumption, her Enthronement, and her Coronation. From many of these Christian art has drawn the subjects of its most renowned works.

The wonderful variety and expressiveness of the titles given to her is also observable. She is

[1] So called from the first line of an old Latin hymn: —
"Stabat Mater Dolorosa
Juxta crucem lachrymosa
Dum pendebat filius."

the Holy Virgin, the Blessed Virgin, the Immaculate Virgin, Our Lady of Peace, Our Lady of Good Counsel, Our Lady of Sorrow, Our Lady of Succor, Our Lady of Good Heart, Our Lady of Mercy, Our Lady of Grace, Our Lady of Hope, Our Lady of Victory, Our Lady of Salvation, Our Lady of the Cradle, Our Lady of the Girdle, Our Guardian Lady, Our Lady of Mount Carmel, Our Lady of Bethlehem, The Queen of Heaven, The Divine Mother, The Mother of Grief, Our Celestial Empress, and she is addressed by other titles more than we can recapitulate. In every considerable place throughout the Roman Catholic world, churches have been consecrated to her, and one particular hour every day, the most thoughtful and tender hour of all, has been set apart for the " Ave Maria."

It may be thought that any citation of these legends is quite unsuited to the purpose of this book, which aims to set forth historical facts and logical arguments bearing on the general thesis in view, while these church stories take us into the region of sentiment and poetry.

But they show us the state of feeling in which originated the popular belief about Christ's mother and his birth. Even at the present day dogmas are more the product of emotion than of reason. How much more was this the case eight and ten centuries ago! On the points referred to, we have inherited a creed from a condition of society which has so long since passed away that we perhaps find it difficult to reproduce it to our imagination; and it is only by the aid of these legends that we can go back to past generations, whose wild and fabulous creations still haunt the domain of Christian thought. For this reason the quotations we propose to make seem germane to our design, and may not detract from its interest.

In translating, then, from the French and Italian, a few of these old legends for our pages, we pass by those that are the best known as being the *motif* of famous pictures, and have taken such as may suggest the variety of services which it was thought the Virgin rendered to her devotees. It will be seen that it was believed that she ministered to the humblest forms of human need.

HOW THE VIRGIN HONORED A SERVANT IN THE MONASTERY.

By the pious care of St. Bernard no less than eight hundred had been gathered under the shadow of the oaks and cloisters of Clairvaux. It was made a valley of milk and honey; and led by him in the way of eternal life, they all had one heart to praise and serve God.

There was with them a menial brother by the name of Didier, a man of the deepest piety, who made a special devotion to the Sainted Virgin, whom he loved with all his heart during the whole course of his life. His duty called him to pass the night of the Assumption in the forest, guarding the sheep of the monastery; and so he could not join in the holy offices in honor of Our Lady. But all night long he ceased not to keep his thoughts turned to heaven, and to salute the Blessed Virgin, adding prayers to prayers, and sighs to sighs. No one won her heart so much as he.

St. Bernard knew all this by express revelation, and the next day, when the holy mysteries of the Assumption had been duly celebrated, he addressed the religious in these words: —

"I do not doubt, my brethren, that you have all offered to our most holy Mother the homage which is her due, and that you will have as a recompense the part which our august and well beloved Sovereign will bestow; but I must in-form you that one of the least of our brethren, who, in the forest guarding our flocks, passed all the joyous night of this grand solemnity, has rendered to the Queen of Heaven an homage, which no one of you, however great has been his devotion, has surpassed in the sight of God and our common Mother. Behold what has raised him above us all!"

And then he related what had been revealed to him. And Didier, at his last hour, saw the Queen of Heaven come in the midst of a cortege of celestial spirits. He heard her call him by name; he saluted her; and she responded with the smile of heaven, and received him to the regions of eternal peace and joy.

HOW THE VIRGIN FREED A SLAVE.

There was once a Christian mother whose son had been carried off by Mussulman pirates, and had long worn the chains of a bitter slavery. She had no money to pay his ransom, and no friends to intercede in his behalf; and in her distress she turned entirely and trustingly to Our Lady of Sorrow.

One day, when her prayer had been fervent, accompanied by alms and fast, the Holy Virgin appeared and said, "What do you wish of me? Why these tears and groans?" And the pious woman replied, "Good Lady, restore to me the child of my love, now in slavery." And the Blessed Virgin said, "Dry up your tears; you shall see your son."

One day soon after, when the mother of the captive was revolving these things in her heart, some one knocked at her door. She opened it, and what was her surprise and joy when she recognized her son. She asked him how he had obtained his freedom. And he said, "One night the Mother of God came to me, and took the irons from my feet and hands and neck, and showed me the way to come to your arms." And on comparing their accounts it appeared that this was on the very night when the Holy Virgin had promised all this to the mother.

THE VIRGIN AND THE LEPER.

In a certain monastery there was a poor lay-brother, whom God had sorely afflicted with leprosy, in order to try him, and that he might lay up by patience and resignation a great sum of merits. He was sequestered from all intercourse with others, and kept in a cell by himself. There succumbing to the might of the hand that was upon him, and feeling the utmost discouragement, he lent an ear to the enemy of all souls, and resolved to throw himself at night into a river hard by.

But he had fear of the dogs that guarded the place every night as soon as it was dark; and so he bethought himself to defer the execution of his plan till Christmas Eve, when no one slept, and the dogs were not on watch. Meanwhile his disease had so disabled him that he now could not walk a step, and hardly could he sustain himself on his feet. Then he tried to drag himself to the water, but this he found impossible.

This poor brother had formerly been a most devout worshiper of the Virgin, and in his extremity she did not forget him. One night she appeared to him, accompanied by many holy angels, and by John, a brother of the monastery. She said, in gentle and loving tones, " My son, do not neglect the service of God; and be not cast down when he chastises you, for like a Father he corrects for their good those whom he loves." When the Holy Virgin had thus comforted this poor leper with sweet words she departed with her angel attendants.

Not long after, some one came to ask the leper if he was in want of anything, and he asked to see Brother John. To him he began to recount his vision; but John said, "I have seen all of which you speak; not with my bodily eyes, but with the eyes of my soul; and the Blessed Virgin when she left you went to the choir of monks, to witness to these servants of God her satisfaction in their chanting the praises of the Most High." Then the leper had no doubt that he had indeed been favored with a celestial visit from the Divine Mother, whose loving counsel he followed, showing ever after heroic patience and resignation, and dying in the most pious and edifying manner.

THE VIRGIN AND THE ARCHITECT.

In the year 324 the Emperor Constantine, among other temples which he consecrated to the Virgin, designed one which should be the most costly, and most worthy of the Blessed Mother of Jesus. So he had enormous columns cut in the quarries, and transported to the chosen place. But what was his surprise to find that through their vast size and length they could not be set on end. In vain for a long time they tried to raise them; all their plans failed, and their labor was lost.

The architect, who was deeply grieved, was one night in bed revolving this difficulty. All at once the Holy Virgin appeared to him and said, "Cease to be sad. I will show you what to do." And so she briefly explained what machines and ropes were to be used, and then added, "Take with you three little children. You will need no more; I will give you help."

When the architect awoke, he recalled his dream, and prepared his towers, his cables, his pulleys, just as she had prescribed; and calling three children from a neighboring school he set to work. Wonderfully the columns arose and took their appointed place, and crowds of people came to see how one man with three little children had done what a thousand arms had in vain attempted.

HOW THE VIRGIN SELECTED A SITE FOR A CHURCH.

In the year 363 the Divine Mother chose to give in Rome a mark of her gracious favor and to confirm her worship by a prodigy. There was then in Rome a powerful and rich Patrician, whose wife had brought him as large an estate as he possessed himself. They were equal in rank, in the gifts of nature, and the graces of the heart, but one joy was wanting. They were childless; and afflicted that they had no heir to their vast fortune, they resolved to devote it all to the Celestial Mother.

One night in the month of August, when the heats are the greatest in Rome, there fell on the Esquiline Hill a quantity of snow, which in the morning was seen to cover the ground. That same night this Patrician, whose name was John, and his wife also, had a dream in which the Holy Virgin appeared to both of them, telling them to construct a temple to her honor on the spot which she would mark with snow.

Early then the next morning John went and recounted the wonderful vision to the Pope, Liberius, who said that he also had had the same revelation. The Pontiff then ordered a procession, and clergy and people went with the chant of hymns and with lighted torches to the Esquiline Hill. Some say the snow had fallen in lines to mark the dimensions of the church. There a temple was built at the expense of the Patrician John and his virtuous wife. At first the church was known by the name of Nostra Donna Delle Neve, Our Lady of the Snow; but afterwards it received the name it bears to this day of Santa Maria Maggiore, and is now one of the largest basilicas of Rome.[1]

HOW THE VIRGIN PLANNED A BATTLE.

For sixty years Italy had been the prey of the Goths, and Theodoric and Totila, kings of those barbarians, had brought that beautiful country to a deplorable state. At length the piety and good works of the Emperor Justinian mounted to the throne of God; and the Queen of Heaven, to whom the emperor was specially devoted, had pleaded with God and had obtained favor.

There was at that time in the army of the emperor a general of small stature and feeble constitution, but of great valor and of signal piety towards the Blessed Mother. One night she appeared to him and traced the plan of a campaign,

[1] "The whole story of the vision, the snow-storm, and the founding of this church, is represented in the mosaics of the thirteenth century still on its façade; and the Pope tracing the foundations in the snow is the subject elsewhere represented in a gilt and silver relief over the altar of the magnificent Borghese chapel in the same basilica." Heman's *History of Ancient Sacred Art*.

and taught him what marches to make, what ambushes to escape, and what positions to fortify.

In everything he followed her counsels; and when the army of Totila was cut to pieces, in 563, on the plains of Tuscany, the celestial Queen herself was seen, as many testified who were there, directing the operations that led to that renowned victory.

THE VIRGIN AND THE MIRACULOUS CANDLE.

In the year 1095 the village of Arras was smitten with the plague, which had commenced in 1089 in Lorraine, and had so much prevailed that that year was called the *pest year*. It endured for a long time, and depopulated parts of France and covered it with grief.

In this extremity the inhabitants of Arras had recourse to the supreme and all powerful *consolatrice* of human sorrow. Processions were made, and prayers the most fervent mounted on the two wings of faith and hope to the throne of the Virgin.

She was not deaf to their supplications. One day as the bishop, Lambert, entered the church at the head of a great procession, all the people saw the Virgin descend from the towers, bearing a miraculous candle, which she placed in the hands of two men, who were mortal enemies, and whom she thus wished to reconcile with each other. They carried it to the bishop, who received it with tears of joy. When it was lighted, it burned one hundred years without consuming or being extinguished; and water into which drops from this candle had fallen was a perfect cure of the pest.

In memory of this a fête was established, and a rich chapel for the miraculous candle was built. Pope Sixtus IV. ordained that an exact narrative of the miracle here wrought should be prepared; and afterwards Pope Clement VIII., by a bull in 1597, accorded indulgences to those who should visit this chapel in Arras.

THE VIRGIN AND THE CISTERCIANS.

In the year 1113 a monk of the religious order of Cistercians, who had a special devotion to the Holy Mother, was favored with an ecstasy in which the heavens were opened to him, and he saw the choirs of angels, and the patriarchs, and the prophets, and the apostles, and the martyrs, and confessors, and various orders of monks, all distinguished by their proper emblems. But, alas, there was not one of his own order there.

With sorrow he turned to the Divine Empress of Heaven and said, "Why, Holy Virgin, do I see none of my order here?" And the august Queen of Heaven replied, "Because the Cistercians to me are so dear, I do not treat them as others; but like to a hen who gathers her brood under her wings, I gather the elect whom your order hath given to the realm of my Son." With these words she opened the ample folds of her mantle, and there was an innumerable company of saints that had belonged to this order.

The monk was overwhelmed with joy. He gave to the Divine Protectress the most fervent thanks; and when his ecstasy ceased, he related the wonderful vision to his Superior.

HOW THE VIRGIN TREATED THE INCREDULITY OF THOMAS.

When the Blessed Mother ascended to heaven in the sight of the apostles, it so happened that Thomas was not present with the rest of the Twelve, but after three days he returned to them. When they related to him the wonderful story of her translation, he doubted and said he would not believe unless he should find her tomb empty. Upon this they showed him the tomb which she had left; and the Holy Virgin, taking pity upon him, threw down from heaven her girdle that this might remove all doubt from his mind.

Thus some perhaps natural impediment to a believing spirit, so often visited with stern rebuke, moved the blessed Mother to tender compassion, and gently won a heart to faith which might otherwise have been driven to unbelief. In the Florentine Gallery is a charming picture by Granacci, representing the Virgin seated on the clouds, and surrounded by a choir of angels, while beneath her is the empty tomb. Thomas is kneeling beside it, and the Virgin drops her girdle down into his hand, which he receives with grateful joy and reverence.

HOW THE VIRGIN MARRIED ST. CATHARINE TO HER SON.

Catharine's father was a brother of Constantine the Great. He died when she was but fourteen years of age, and left her with his kingdom, heiress of immense wealth. From her infancy she had been the wonder of all, for her grace of person and gifts of mind; and when she became queen she despised the cares of royal splendor, and gave herself to study.

The nobles of the country begged that she would be pleased to take a husband who should assist her in the government of the kingdom, and lead forth their armies to war. "And what manner of man is this that I must marry?" she asked. And they said to her: "You are our most sovereign lady and queen, and it is well known to all that you possess four most notable gifts: the first is, you have the most noble blood in the whole world; the second is, that you are the greatest heiress whom we know; the third is, that in science and wisdom you surpass all others; and the fourth is, that in beauty none can be compared with you. Wherefore we beseech you that these good gifts, with which the great God hath endowed you beyond all creatures, may move you to take a lord to your husband who shall be not unworthy of your choice."

And then the queen said: "If God hath wrought so great virtues in us, we are bound to love him and to please him; and he that shall be my husband, and the lord of my heart, must have also notable gifts: he must be of so noble blood that all men shall worship him, and so great that I shall never think that I have made him king, and so rich that he shall surpass all others in wealth, and so full of beauty that the angels of God shall desire to behold him, and so benign that he can gladly forgive all offenses done unto him. If you can find me such an one I will take him for my husband and the lord of my heart."

Then all her lords and friends looked upon each other and said, "Such an one as she hath described there never was and never shall be."

Now the Virgin Mary appeared out of heaven and sent a message by a holy hermit to the young Queen Catharine, to tell her that the husband she desired was the Virgin's Son, who was the King of glory, and Lord of all power and might. And when Catharine slept, the Blessed Virgin appeared to her in a dream, accompanied by her Divine Son, and with them a noble company of saints and angels. And the Lord smiled upon her and held out his hand, and plighted his troth to her, and put a ring on her finger, and when she awoke the ring was there, and thenceforth she regarded herself as the betrothed of Christ.

We must quote no more of these legends, though hundreds of them might be given. There was no form of sorrow, or trouble, or need, which the Divine Mother could not help. No doubt some of these tales were as much fictions as, in Disraeli's story, was the reported appearance of the Virgin to save the life of Lothair;[1] yet many

---

[1] "That some of the Christian legends were deliberate forgeries can scarcely be questioned. The principle of pious fraud appeared to justify this mode of working on the popular mind. It was admitted and avowed. To deceive into Christianity was so valuable a service as to hallow deceit itself. But the largest portion was probably the natural birth of that imaginative excitement which quickens its day-dreams and nightly visions into reality." Milman.

"There are other avenues, more trodden than the narrow way of reason, by which opinions enter the mind. What impresses the imagination, affects the feelings, and is blended with habitual association, is received by the generality as true. Fables however absurd, conceptions however irrational, even unmeaning forms of words, which have been early presented to the mind, and with which it has been long conversant, make as vivid an impression upon it as realities, and assume their character. No opinions inhere more strongly than those about which the reason is not exercised; for they are unassailable by argument. Nor shall we find it hard to conceive, nor regard it as a very extraordinary fact, that the fables respecting the mother of our Lord and our Lord himself have been credited, as well as the doctrine of transubstantiation. Undoubtedly, the world has grown wiser; or rather a small portion of the world has grown wiser, and we may hope the light will become less troubled, steadier, and brighter, and spread itself more widely." Norton's *Genuineness of the Gospels*, vol. iii., p. 274.

of them may have been mostly founded on some fact, and grateful and devout imaginations gave them the form in which they have come down to us. They are the language of wonder, of love and joy, of unreasoning and highly wrought exaltation of feeling; and those who told these stories and those who heard them no more thought of asking if they were true, than we think of asking for the chemical properties of the peach or the grape whose flavor we enjoy. These legends belonged to an age which will never return, but to which they were as much fitted as baby-talk is fitted to infancy, and as our stammering intellectualism is fitted to the age in which we live; and of two things we hardly know which is the most absurd, to criticise them according to our modern ideas, or to insist that we shall now believe them just as they were believed a few centuries ago.

A few centuries ago! How strange it seems that we stand so near the time when they were the intellectual and spiritual nourishment of our ancestors! The Reformation has banished them from our sympathies and affections as much, as Mrs. Jameson very justly says, "as if they were antecedent to the fall of Babylon, or related to the religion of Zoroaster." But the purpose for which we have quoted them will not be overlooked. It has been to show how much they served to fix deeply in the convictions and hearts of the people these misinterpretations which made Mary the Mother of God.

The subject of the " Immaculate Conception " connects itself here with our general topic. It is easy to see the sort of reasoning which led to that dogma. After the seventh century it was said, if Mary be the Mother of God, she must have been a pure shrine for his dwelling; and therefore must have been free both from original and acquired sinfulness. " It was argued," as Mrs. Jameson says, " that God never suffered any temple of his to be profaned: he had even promulgated severe ordinances to preserve his sanctuary inviolate. How much more to him was *that* temple, that tabernacle built by no human hands, in which he had condescended to dwell! Nothing was impossible to God; it lay therefore in his power to cause his Mother to come absolutely pure and immaculate into the world. Being in his power, could any earnest worshiper of the Virgin for a moment suppose that for one so favored it would not be done." Did not the Song of Solomon say, in a text which Romish theologians applied to the Virgin, "Thou art all fair, my love; there is no spot in thee"? Canticles iv. 7.

Yet St. Thomas Aquinas said, "If Mary was conceived without sin, then she does not need the redemption of Christ." And St. Bonaventura said, "We ought to beware lest by the honor we ascribe to the Mother, we derogate from the glory of the Son, and to remember that the Creator stands higher than any creature. We could by no means affirm, without impiety, that the Holy Virgin had no need of redemption."

But in time this difficulty was adroitly avoided. The hypothesis was framed that Jesus freed his mother from sin beforehand, so that she no longer stood in need of the general redemption.

For several centuries, however, there was a sharp discussion on this point, and the Franciscans and Dominicans were divided in opinion. At length Sixtus IV., who had been a Franciscan, issued a papal decree in favor of the dogma. A form of service was composed, in 1496, for the festival of the Conception. But this was not formally instituted until 1617, when Paul V. issued a bull forbidding any one to teach and preach against the Immaculate Conception. This was received in Spain particularly, where the Franciscans were held in great esteem, and where no less than one hundred and fifty books had been written on the subject, in a frenzy of religious joy; and tournaments, bull-fights, and banquets attested the triumph of the votaries of the Virgin.

The exact definition of this dogma as an article of faith was not authoritatively given until 1854, when Pio Nono assembled three hundred prelates at Rome, and decreed with great pomp in St. Peter's, " That the most Blessed Virgin Mary, in the first instant of her conception, was preserved free from all stain of original sin by the singular grace and privilege of Almighty God, and through the merits of Jesus Christ." A tasteless monument in memory of this event was erected in 1857, in the Piazza di Spagna at Rome, the monument we have before referred to, and large marble tablets, recording the names of those who assisted at this decree, have been ostentatiously placed in the chancel of St. Peter's.

CHAPTER XI.

CONCLUSION.

THE point we have been discussing in this volume does not relate to an abstract subject of no practical importance. It intimately concerns our mode of conceiving of the Master of Christians, and our ability to understand and love him. The prevailing views push him aside into a region of mystery and shadows, and make him a mythical demi-god. They take away our revered Elder Brother, "and we know not where they have laid him." It seems as if in sorrowful tones we hear him say, " Have I been so long time with you and yet hast thou not known me?"

On the other hand, if we think of him as born of human parents, tempted in all respects as we are, receiving, as his intellectual and spiritual nature unfolded, a supply of God's illuminating grace which has distinguished him from every other being on earth, we have a view not only in harmony with the Scriptures, but intelligible to our understanding, and welcome to our heart. This makes Jesus, what he so often called himself, the Son of Man, but no less the Son of God.

In their anxiety to mark something superhuman in Jesus, theologians, as it seems to us, have applied to his body expressions which are true only of his soul. Thus Neander says on the subject of the miraculous conception: "If we conceive the manifestation of Christ to have been a supernatural communication of the Divine nature for the moral renewal of man, this conception itself, apart from any historical accounts, would lead us to form some notion of the beginning of his humble life that would harmonize with it. He entered into history not as a part of its offspring but as a higher element. Whatever has its origin in the natural course of humanity must bear the stamp of humanity, and share in the sinfulness that stains it. It was impossible that the second Adam, the Divine progenitor of a new and heavenly race, could derive his origin from the first Adam, in the ordinary course of nature. And so our own idea of Christ compels us to admit that two factors, the one natural, and the other supernatural, were coefficient in his entrance into human life; and this too although we may be unable *a priori* to state how that entrance was accomplished."[1]

But if in order to have a sinless being it be necessary that his body should be removed from the idea of earthly parentage, the argument requires that the mother should have no share in its production.

We admit that Jesus was above "the ordinary course of humanity," was a "communication of the Divine nature for the moral renewal of man;" but what has this to do with the origin of his *body?* The Divine nature entered into history as a higher element through Christ's soul; and so we recognize the two factors, the human organization and the divine illumination; but no proof is offered to show that the latter cannot have connection with the former; and who are we who talk about the "impossibility" of this? Such a connection is confessed if the mother had any share in the formation of the body of Jesus.

Olshausen follows in the same strain. Arguing for the miraculous birth he says: "If we recognize in Christ an actual incarnation of the Word of God, then the narration of his supernatural generation, so far from astonishing us,

[1] *Life of Christ.*

seems for the Saviour specially natural and befitting. The very idea of a Saviour requires that in him there should be manifested something higher, something heavenly, that cannot be derived from what exists in human nature."

Yes, we see in Jesus "something higher, something heavenly," and above ordinary human nature. But all this belonged to his soul. What kind of a body shall we attribute to Jesus if not a human body?

This inherited corruption of man's nature to which both Neander and Olshausen refer, and on which countless other writers so much insist — the dogma which has been age after age handed down in the Romish and Evangelical churches — who can refrain from asking, What is it? What does it amount to? Is it a deeply fixed stain, ineffaceable except by miracle? Have these churches really believed that it can be cut off only by supernatural means?

Every reader knows that these churches have not believed this. They have held that the transmitted stain, whatever it was, could be removed in the easiest mode in the world. Baptismal regeneration, as they teach, puts it all away. The corruption of Adam, original sin, is abolished by the water of baptism. So that now a priest can any day do what God could not do except by a stupendous departure from the laws of Nature.

In a different school of thought from the above-named writers, we find Professor Norton arguing for the miraculous conception in the following manner: "Nothing could have served more effectually to relieve Jesus from that interposition and embarrassment in the performance of his high mission, to which he would have been exposed on the part of his parents if born in the common course of nature. It took him from their control, and made them feel that in regard to him they were not to interfere with the purposes of God."

Perhaps the reader will think, as we do, that this is finding reasons for a previous conclusion. It often happens in such cases that the reasons do not tally with the facts. There is no evidence to show that Jesus was in the least taken from the control of his parents; or that anything occurred in regard to his birth to impress his family circle with feelings of awe. On the other hand we are told that "his brethren did not believe in him," John vii. 5; and even thought him mad, Mark iii. 21.

CONCLUSION.

In view of some historical notices, in a former chapter, of sacerdotal celibacy, the remark of Milman, defending the miraculous conception, "that it has consecrated sexual purity," seems amazing. In order to remove all thoughts of Christ's birth from the circle of nature, ten thousand engines for centuries have played their dirty streams upon the relation of the sexes, and instead of consecrating its purity seem rather to have covered it with filth.

We find another opinion of Milman which we quote with more satisfaction. In referring to what he calls "the poetical and imaginative incidents of the birth of Christ," he very justly ascribes to them a vast influence over the thoughts and affections of mankind. "This language of poetic incident, and, if I may so speak, of imagery, interwoven as it was with the popular belief, infused into the hymns, the services, the ceremonial of the Church, introduced in material representation by painting and sculpture, has become the vernacular tongue of Christendom, universally intelligible, and responded to by the human heart throughout these many centuries."

No doubt this is true; and we may well be thankful for it; and be glad that this language of poetic imagery is long to hold its influence over the human heart. It will be an influence all the greater when we see it as the language of poetry, and no strange questioning of what it means, and dim shadows of prodigious and incredible things, shall perplex and darken the mind.

So also in our arguments with unbelievers what a help it will be to shut off all objections naturally and inevitably arising from the misinterpretation of the records of the birth of Jesus, and to feel no longer bound to defend the traditions which originated hundreds of years after that event. We shall not then think of proving Christ's divinity by such arguments as the virginity of Mary and the continence of Joseph.

Moreover, what a satisfaction it will be to know that we can trace the footsteps of our religious faith quite back to the simplicity of the first preachers of the Gospel. Nothing is clearer than that much of our theological diction originated in those muddled politico-dialectic disputes of the fourth and fifth centuries. Language is a record which nothing can falsify. Two thousand years hence an historian, meeting in old books the first words about railroads, will know that those expressions originated in the first half of the nineteenth century, and were entirely unknown before. With a like certainty we know where much of our religious terminology came from, and are sure it does not come from the Gospels, nor from the writings of the apostles.

No one who has read Macaulay's review of Ranke's "History of the Popes" will forget the few striking paragraphs which show that in Europe Protestantism has made no geographical advances since the first impulse of the Reformation, while Catholicism has regained some of the ground it then lost. With equal truth it may be said that theology has made hardly any progress since the first fresh days of the Reformers, while many of the dogmas of the Roman Catholic Church have been more strongly intrenched in the very bosom of Protestantism. We have continued to drink the water of life, not as it flowed direct from the Divine fountain which God opened for our healing, but as it has trickled through turbid papal channels. Perhaps it will one day be seen that in order to get into the true current of apostolical descent, we must go back to a time before a corrupt side-stream from Egypt, by fraud and violence, flooded the Church of Christ.[1]

[1] "It cannot be regarded as a strange event that, at a time

In looking back to the epoch which succeeded that of the apostles, it is only too evident that it was marked by a constant degeneracy both in intelligence and spirituality. The lofty mind and the great soul of Jesus lifted up all who had personally known him. His inspiring influence to a large degree survived through a few following generations. But with the lapse of time it was much weakened. This is the general effect of the withdrawal of a great mental and spiritual guide. The reaction is usually proportioned to his superiority.

When, then, we come down to the fourth century, and the immediately subsequent centuries, the men we meet in history are widely different from Paul, and Peter, and John. Indeed, what a contrast! Petty questions, petty subtleties, petty superstitions, petty strifes, are now the rage. Who can imagine the apostles going forth on their missionary journeys as carrying with them a splinter of the true cross, a thorn from

when most believers could not read, tradition should acquire an authority above the real record of the Gospel; and of tradition it has been justly said that it is like the parasite plant which at first clings to and rests on the tree, which it gradually overspreads with its own foliage, till little by little it weakens and completely smothers it." Whately's *Kingdom of Heaven*, Philadelphia edit., p. 53.

the bloody crown, a thread from the seamless garment, a paring from one of the finger-nails on the pierced hands? When men had lost an ability to comprehend the real significance of what Jesus had taught, these superstitious and perhaps counterfeit relics became everything.

At that time, too, a syllable more or less would kindle fury, and make multitudes fly to arms. On an insignificant question about a formula, excommunication and banishment were suspended. There was a race of narrow minds and hard hearts. The tide of Christian intelligence and Christian virtue hardly ever ebbed lower than with them. Yet they gave a shape to the Gospel which not only the Catholic but the Protestant world has accepted as its clearest and final word. If human authority be needed to interpret and verify Christianity, how astounding that we should look for it among the ambitious and corrupt pettifoggers of the epoch referred to.

The times in which we live seem favorable in one respect for important reforms in theology. It would be absurd to found many hopes on any one sect, for none has a monopoly of this work. The best encouragement is in the large number of generous-minded and scholarly men of all denominations who feel uneasy under sectarian restraints, and long to see eye to eye those with whom they know they have a spiritual alliance. Probably there has never been a day when this number was larger than now.

Still the bondage of sect is wide-spread, and often overwhelming. One might be surprised to count up the number and power of material interests that are pledged to some old creed. Funds, churches, periodicals, theological schools, countless religious and social organizations, partisan leadership, hopes of advancement, means of daily bread — all are at stake, in numberless cases, upon the retention of certain formulas of faith. The sermons, the habits of thought, the exhortations, the gestures, the roll of the eye, the shake of the head, of thousands of preachers are adjusted to a certain belief; and to overthrow that is to take away their stock in trade. Theological schools seem to answer the end of camp-life to raw soldiers, that is, to break down the will of many to the command of a few; and so it is that we go on repeating from generation to generation the same old rattling and hollow forms, and all improvement in theology has a hard fight against these resisting forces.

It would denote extreme verdancy to suppose that any churches are now formed to encourage higher conceptions of truth. Who does not know that their corporate strength is always given to the defense or diffusion of a preconceived creed? Hence Dr. Arnold of Rugby said, " In the great end of a church all churches are now greatly deficient. The life of these societies has long been gone. They do not help the individual in holiness. This in itself is evil enough; but it is monstrous that they should pretend to fetter where they do not assist." [1]

It will not be strange if it should be said by some that it is the design of this book to lower our idea of Jesus, and to reduce him to the measure of our humanity. We feel sure that no one who reads this work would willingly bear false witness. Our design is very far from that here named. We think that we have the highest idea of his person. In his life we recognize the advent of a new spirit, a new power, into the world, coming direct from God. Yet we believe it works in an organic connection with the natural, so that while the chain of cause and effect is not broken, a higher influence mingles in the

[1] *Life of Dr. Arnold,* vol. ii., p. 57.

links of that chain, and operates in the circle of human instrumentality. And we hold to this view, and commend it to others, because it seems to bring us nearer to our Divine Teacher and Guide.

If we look to other branches of inquiry, how plainly we see the need of fresh, independent investigation to emancipate us from long inherited errors. The other day, as we were turning over the leaves of a book relating to the history of medical opinions, we were astonished at the groundless theories, the puerile absurdities, the superstitious *nostrums*, that had long been handed down from the dark ages, and implicitly adopted, generation after generation, as the substance of therapeutic science. This enormous mass of error has almost tempted some eminent medical writers to wish that all traditional maxims and remedies could be annihilated, so that there might be a fresh study of each case.

This is the fact where the point to be investigated touches our external senses, and requires for its successful prosecution only good eyes, good ears, and unbiased, trained habits of careful discrimination. How incredible, then, to suppose there have been no inherited errors in a sphere of thought above our external senses, in the science of theology, in dogmas framed in times of gross ignorance, and transmitted from father to son unaltered for ten or fifteen centuries.

A spirit of investigation, which has reconstructed all other branches of knowledge, will some time break up the petrified crusts of theology. A silent change is even now going on, far more deep and fundamental than the great revolution which we call the Protestant Reformation, and which, if it were allied, as then, to questions of dynasties and state interests, would produce even greater convulsions. Thinking men everywhere see that there must be a readjustment of our ideas of God, of Christ, of the Bible, in order to bring them into truer relations with the advancement of the age.

We have failed altogether in the object kept in view in this book if the mind of the reader be not impressed with a sense of the wrong which the ages have inflicted upon Jesus. Of course they have sought to honor him, but it was been in a way which he would have forbidden. High sounding titles have shut him out of the sphere of human sympathies. His murderers mockingly said, "Hail, King of the Jews!" in after times his friends sincerely applied to him like inflated epithets; but the effect was in both cases the same — to alienate from him human affections.

And to whom were these estranging phrases applied? It was to him who loved man most tenderly, who came closer to the human heart than any other soul known on earth, whose chosen title was *Son of Man*, who declared that the humblest child who did the will of God was his mother and sister and brother. Such was he who has been lifted up on a pedestal above our clear vision, has been surrounded by mists and clouds, and has been made the object of a conventional adulation instead of a natural love.

If we have any right sympathy with the mind of Jesus, we must see that he would have infinitely preferred that love. The world has defrauded him. We have defrauded ourselves, also, of a mighty aid. Fellowship with such a lofty human soul is one of the most quickening helps to draw us up to his transcendent height.

No doubt for the humanity of Jesus the early Christians had a sympathy which, with those who succeeded them, was weakened and nearly

CONCLUSION.

lost. To be convinced of this we have only to mark the way in which the first disciples spoke of him. Whom did St. Peter preach on the day of Pentecost? "Jesus of Nazareth, a man approved of God." Acts ii. 22. Whom did St. Paul declare to be the one Mediator between God and man? "The man Christ Jesus." 1 Timothy ii. 5. Whom did St. Paul say God had sent into the world? "His son, made of a woman." Galatians iv. 4. By whom came, according to St. Paul, the sure hope of a future life? "By man came the resurrection from the dead." 1 Corinthians xv. 21. In his memorable speech at Athens, whom did St. Paul announce as assisting at the judgment of the last day? "God will judge the world in righteousness by that man whom he hath ordained." Acts xvii. 31. In his sermon at Antioch of Pisidia St. Paul preached the forgiveness of sins; but through whom? "Be it known unto you, men and brethren, that through this man is preached forgiveness of sins." Acts xiii. 38. And, finally, when the writer of the Epistle to the Hebrews set forth the true and acceptable offering, in what terms did he allude to Jesus? "This man, after he had offered one sacrifice for sins, forever sat down on the right hand of God." Hebrews x. 12.

Thus it was the manhood of Jesus to which constant reference was made — a humanity with which they could sympathize, while they rejoiced that our human nature was made the vehicle of God's grace, and was the antetype and prophecy of what man, in some future age, was to become.

But this style of speaking of Jesus soon ceased. We find nothing like it in all the literature that succeeded apostolic times. Then came the exegesis, still in vogue, of two natures, between which, it was supposed, Jesus and his apostles prevaricated. Men's hearts were thus turned away from an earnest love of a brother to empty boasts of a demi-god. What a confirmation is here of the leading view of this book!

On all sides we hear complaints of prevailing indifference to the great themes which in other times have most profoundly moved the human mind. Is no part of this indifference attributable to the divorce between modern intelligence and an outgrown theology? To what length may the antagonism extend? Is not a higher plane of free and thorough criticism one of the great needs of our times? Are there not many subjects which should be brought before the bar of a criticism like that? Is not here the remedy for existing and menacing evils? Aware of many imperfections in the work which we here close, and not doubting but that in some points we may have made mistakes, we are yet conscious that it has been written in the interest of a true religion, — of a profound reverence for its verities and hopes.

www.ingramcontent.com/pod-product-compliance
Lightning Source LLC
Chambersburg PA
CBHW020858230426
43666CB00008B/1226